Teaching the Postmodern: Fiction and Theory

Brenda K. Marshall

ROUTLEDGE

New York and London

Published in 1992 by

Routledge
An imprint of Routledge, Chapman and Hall, Inc.
29 West 35 Street
New York, NY 10001

Published in Great Britain by

Routledge
11 New Fetter Lane
London EC4P 4EE

Library of Congress Cataloging-in-Publication Data and British Library Cataloguing
in Publication Data also available.

ISBN 0-415-90454-4 (HB)
ISBN 0-415-90455-2 (PB)

Teaching the Postmodern

Contents

Acknowledgments

Portions of Chapter 5 appeared in different form in the author's article, "Meta(hi)story: Timothy Findley's *Famous Last Words*," *The International Fiction Review* 16:1 (Winter 1989).

I would like to thank R. Radhakrishnan, Dale Peterson, and Don Eric Levine for their many comments and conversations about earlier versions of this book. Concerning any advice I neglected to heed, I ask for their patience.

My thanks also go to Linda Hutcheon for her generous encouragement, without which this book may never have been finished.

Most importantly, I thank the following persons: my best friend, whose constant encouragement motivates me; my favorite fellow scholar, whose intellectual demands and questions stimulate my work; my live-in counselor, whose consistently good advice contains within it space for my own whimsy; and my partner, who provides the reason for most of the good things I do. Thank you, Valerie.

Introduction

différance

historiography   genealogy

     Morrison   context

Kristeva   deconstruction

                    ex-centric

structuralism   history

   language   Wolf

                        Barthes

         counter-memory   history

    metafiction   language

       Carter   ideology

      parody   play

          de Lauretis   intertextuality

subject position   Derrida

history   Foucault

               feminism

                    language

    Rushdie   Marxism

              critical revisiting

poststructuralism

text   work   Hutcheon

   Coetzee   language

Althusser   historiographic metafiction

They shuffle uncomfortably in a shared space, rub shoulders angrily, eye each other suspiciously, laugh, and look for the door. There is none. They are neither outside nor inside. Sometimes they clasp hands in recognition, and then begin to dispute. Each has a definition, each resists definition, each defines the other. Each is a node within a multi-dimensional network, one of uncountable nodes. From each node project threads which tangle with the threads of other nodes. Together they do not make a tapestry. No coherent picture emerges because there is no one who is not part of the network, there is no position from which to step back and take a look, no one sitting on the other end of Archimedes' lever. This is not chaos, this is not anarchy, this is not entropy, although it may be chaotic, anarchic, entropic. There is sense here, but not safe sense. Sense made here is limited, local, provisional, and always critical. Self-critical. That is sense within the postmodern moment. That is the postmodern.

The word has been spoken. Books close, eyes close. Oh dear, that again. But don't worry: I'm not here to get it right, once and for all. No, *that* wouldn't be very postmodern. Rather, this book is designed to present certain shared concerns of theorists (often post-structuralist) and of fiction writers who are working within and thus reflect what I call the postmodern moment. Some of these concerns of the postmodern have to do with language: with how we constitute and are constituted by language; with the power of interpretation of language (who takes control of meaning). Another concern has to do with an emphasis on difference rather than on Identity: for example, people (and societies) are perceived of as sites of difference, and not as centers from which pure knowledge emanates and to which absolute Truth may be made known. This notion, like everything else, must be historicized. That many contemporary artists (I will be speaking specifically of fiction writers) and theorists share a common discursive space in which these concerns are raised, and that these concerns make enough sense to us today for us to formulate them, is one indication of the postmodern moment: a moment which demands an awareness of being-within a way of thinking. Designed as an introduction to some of the basic concerns of the postmodern, this text functions as the toe put in to test the water, followed by an introductory swimming lesson. Because these waters can get pretty deep.

If this is an introduction, then, the next step should be to define 'postmodernism'. There are a great many books and articles which begin with or include a series of definitions and a study of the term's progression. See, for example, Foster (1983), Hutcheon (1983, 1988), Huyssen (1984), Jameson (1984), Kroker and Cook (1986), Lyotard (1984), McCaffery (1986), Ross (1988), Spanos (1987), Trachtenberg, et al. (1985). You will not find total agreement, but you will find moments where the definitions bump into and nod at one another.

One of the results of seeing the postmodern moment as an awareness of being-within a way of thinking is the recognition that such an awareness disallows the speaker (the subject) the comfort of absolutely naming the terms of that moment. Naming must occur from a position 'outside' of a moment, and it always indicates an attempt to control. Crucial to an understanding of the postmodern moment is the recognition that there is no 'outside' from which to 'objectively' name the present. The postmodern moment is an awareness of being-within, first, a language, and second, a particular historical, social, cultural framework. That is, we know we are within a particular framework or paradigm of thought, even if we cannot say with certainty how that paradigm works. Only from a fictional, removed, and separate point of perspective do we name (identify) the framework or paradigm within which people have lived in the past. 'Fictional' is the operative word here. There can be no such thing as objectivity: all of our definitions and understanding of all that has come before us must pass through our historical, social, cultural being, as well as through our language—all of which precede us and constitute us, even as we insist on our own control (Foucault, 1970). That does not mean that we are paralyzed or helpless; rather, it means that we give up the luxury of absolute Truths, choosing instead to put to work local and provisional truths. In short, we go about the work of living and maneuvering within this postmodern moment.

Look at an example of why we cannot exactly define 'postmodernism' within the postmodern moment. We begin our definition with "Postmodernism is . . ." and are already in trouble. We cannot get very far without "*is.*" Language lays a trap: it says something must *be*, always *be*. Thus, by attempting to define postmodernism, it is given primary ontological status, suggesting that there is "a Post-Modernist essence that precedes post-modern practice" (Radhakrishnan, 1983, 33), that it has some transcendental Identity. We thus must bracket [is], or put it 'under erasure' when it follows 'postmodernism' (Derrida, 1976). The bracket/erasure is a trick, of course, but a useful trick if it helps us to remember the way language maneuvers us into complicity.

Postmodernism is about language. About how it controls, how it determines meaning, and how we try to exert control through language. About how language restricts, closes down, insists that it stands for some *thing*. Postmodernism is about how 'we' are defined within that language, and within specific historical, social, cultural matrices. It's about race, class, gender, erotic identity and practice, nationality, age, ethnicity. It's about difference. It's about power and powerlessness, about empowerment, and about all the stages in between and beyond and unthought of. Postmodernism is about the everything that's come before that shows up in the detritus and the brilliance and the everyday of now. It's about those threads that we trace, and trace, and trace. But not to a conclusion. To increased knowledge, yes. But never to innocent knowledge. To better understanding, yes. But never to pure insight. Postmodernism is about history. But not the kind of 'History' that lets us think we can know the past. History in the postmodern moment becomes histories and questions. It asks: Whose history gets told? In whose name? For what purpose? Postmodernism is about histories not told, retold, untold. History as it never was. Histories forgotten, hidden, invisible, considered unimportant, changed, eradicated. It's about the refusal to see history as linear, as leading straight up to today in some recognizable pattern—all set for us to make sense of. It's about chance. It's about power. It's about information. And more information. And more. And. And that's just a little bit about what postmodernism [is].

From what I have said so far, it's clear that we need to bracket the 'ism' in postmodern[ism] as well. The 'ism' suggests that here is something complete, unified, totalized. Such a dream of unity is critiqued within the postmodern moment as a false vision of mastery. The word postmodernism, as I use it, does not refer to a period or a 'movement'. It isn't really an 'ism'; it isn't really a thing. It's a moment, but more a moment in logic than in time. Temporally, it's a space. It is like Jacques Derrida's *différance* (see Chapter 2)—a space where meaning takes place, or like Michel Foucault's 'event' (see Chapter 5)—a moment of rupture, of change. The word 'postmodern' is often used synonymously with 'contemporary': postmodernism then becomes equated with an 'anything goes', ahistorical, apolitical, pluralistic creed. Such a position would be, of course, socially and politically naive and untenable. That is not what the postmodern moment refers to. Although our contemporary culture has evidenced enough flashes of the postmodern moment for it to be an increasingly familiar term, we are not living in a period identified 'totally' as postmodern. There are postmodern moments in *Tristram Shandy* and in *Don Quixote* (Spanos, 1987); there is nothing postmodern about *Newsweek* or the fiction of John Jakes. The postmodern moment is not something that is to be defined chronologically; rather, it is a rupture in our consciousness. Its definition lies in change and chance, but it has everything to do with how we read the present, as well as how we read the past. It is of this world, and thus, political. Listen to Radhakrishnan (1983) when he says of the postmodern event:

> it does and will make a difference in the arena of worldly practices, provided it is elaborated nonidentically and in conjunction with the many micrological processes that constitute socio-economic and political reality. (34)

Perhaps I seem overly concerned with brackets and erasures, with the difficulties of naming. But the traditional process of naming—a belief in the identity of things with names, so that 'reality' may be known absolutely—provides a space of interrogation for postmodernism, which asks: whose 'reality' is to be represented through this process of naming? The power-of-the-name bogs down discussions of postmodernism, as theorists question the incompatibility of 'post' and 'modo' within the same term. Or as theorists, in limiting the term to a stage following Modernism, dispute the various definitions of 'modernism' that are possible. But, such attempts to name are also necessary, as Radhakrishnan (1983) points out:

> The very term "Post-Modernism" is a necessary mis-
> nomer; a misnomer, since it attempts to "periodize" a
> break, and necessary, since the language of the break has
> initially to mention and problematize its immediate an-
> tecedent before it commences its own projects. (34)

Radhakrishnan goes on to say that the postmodern event inaugurates "reality as maverick, local and regional, and discontinuous" (1983, 34) by interrogating the logic of naming and representation. That is, to refuse to accept as 'natural' the one-to-one mimetic relationship of things with words, for example, is to identify the concept of nam-ing as an act of will, of power (see Chapter 2). Jean-François Lyotard in *The Postmodern Condition* (1984) makes a similar point about reality as local and regional when he defines *postmodern* as "an incredulity toward metanarratives" (xxiv), toward those grand stories or explanations which make sense of the world according to one overarching truth. The postmodern moment resists totalizations, ab-solute Identity, absolute Truths. It does, however, believe in the use-value of identit*ies* and local and contingent truths.

The critique of totalizations is also one of the areas of critique of poststructuralism. Are poststructuralism and postmodernism, then, synonymous? Not at all. But there exist many parallels and shared concerns. For example, poststructuralism uses, and then cri-tiques structuralism, which posits that meaning is determined by and within systems or structures, just as postmodernism uses and then abuses the structures and values it critiques. The structuralist tenet that meaning is determined by difference (for example, we identify 'hot' through its relationship to cold, i.e., 'not-cold') is compatible with the postmodern moment, although the drive toward closure indicated by this bipolar logic is not. The related poststructuralist move is to work with this emphasis on difference, showing not only how our logic is based on binary difference (hot/cold, inside/outside, self/other) but that the terms are always representative of a hierarchy—inside is superior to outside, self is superior to other. Whereas structuralism's drive is toward closure, poststructuralism resists closure with its emphasis on textuality and intertextuality. Poststructuralism emphasizes our relation to and dependence on language. But within poststructuralist discourse there are debates, disagreements, dialogues, all coming from theorists from varying positions and with widely varying agendas. Poststructuralists share an interest in the constituting aspects of language—how it defines us as much as we define it; how it precedes our awareness of it, so that we are born into and thus shaped by the language which we like to think we contol. But 'poststructuralist' refers more to a paradigm of study than it does to a field: there are poststructuralist psychoanalysts, poststructuralist historians, philosophers, linguists, literary critics, feminists, Marxists, and so forth. Each theorist uses particular poststructuralist critiques and ideas toward a particular agenda. Poststructuralism then is an overly large umbrella term for a methodology, a way of bringing certain tools to intellectual puzzlings.

Some critics speak of poststructuralism and postmodernism as if they were identical or homologous. They are not. Others point out that "poststructuralism is primarily a discourse of and about modernism" (Huyssen, 1984, 37–38; see also Ross, 1988, vii–xviii). Such a linking of poststructuralism to modernism is, to some degree, accurate. The genealogy of poststructuralist theory includes Marx, Freud, Nietzsche, and Saussure (Ross, 1988, ix). And the literary texts worked on by many poststructuralists are also the classic modernists (Flaubert, Proust, Mallarmé, Joyce, Brecht) (Huyssen, 1984, 39). My position, however, is that it is only from within the postmodern moment that the questions and concerns poststructuralists bring to and through these modernists can make 'sense' today. That is, the poststructuralist does not simply refer to or repeat the modernists; rather, s/he interrogates them for a specific purpose within the postmodern móment. In Andrew Ross's words:

> Increasingly, then, the claims of poststructuralism have been placed in a larger context, or "condition," of which they have been seen equally as a symptom and as a determining cause. This larger condition—postmodernism—addresses a whole range of material conditions that are no longer consonant with the dominant rationality of modernism and its technological commitment to finding *solutions* in every sphere of social and cultural life. What we think of as the "postmodern condition" speaks to a complex conjuncture of conditions. For example, it encompasses the vestigial personal revolutions in self-liberation and communal participation initiated by the countercultural movements of the sixties *just as* it entails the dramatic, postwar restructuring of capitalism in the West and in the multinational global economy; it involves the everyday effects of the new media and communication technology *as well as* the great redistribution of power, population, and wealth that has accompanied the new structures of commodity production. (1988, x)

In other words: only within the postmodern moment do the questions raised by poststructuralists have currency. Moreover, these poststructuralist concerns and questions—about language, texts, interpretation, subjectivity, for example—specifically lend themselves to larger historical, social, and cultural questions which inhabit the postmodern moment. Thus, poststructuralism provides many of the tools used for the decidedly political and historical questions of the postmodern moment.

For instance, it is a form of postmodern fiction, historiographic metafiction (see Chapter 5), that combines poststructuralist theoretical tools with fictional narrative strategies to bring to the fore historical interrogations, and thus responds to the appeal below by Huyssen (1984):

> it is time to abandon that dead-end dichotomy of politics and aesthetics which for too long has dominated ac-

counts of modernism, including the aestheticist trend
within poststructuralism. The point is not to eliminate
the productive tension between the political and the aesthetic, between history and the text, between engage-
ment and the mission of art. The point is to heighten
that tension, even to rediscover it and bring it back into
focus in the arts as well as in criticism. (52)

Linda Hutcheon, who has coined the term 'historiographic metafiction,' answers that this is precisely the role of postmodernist art
which, by implicitly contesting "such concepts as aesthetic originality
and textual closure . . . offers a new model for mapping the borderland
between art and the world" (1988, 23).

I have been speaking of the relationship between poststructuralist
theory and postmodernism. Do I mean to suggest that all theory
within the postmodern moment is postmodern? Not at all. For example, on the one hand, the work of Louis Althusser, a Marxist, has
been read as compatible with the postmodern moment, specifically
in terms of his historicizing of the notion of subjectivity in reference
to ideology (Althusser, 1971), and more generally in terms of his
method of posing questions about the historicity of change, ruptures,
breaks (Radhakrishnan, 1990). On the other hand, a case cannot be
made for traditional Marxism, however, as being synonymous, or even
comfortable with the postmodern moment. Marxism, with its di-
alectic, and thus progressive, theory of history, and with its totalizing
representation of society as defined by class struggle, is one of the
master narratives toward which postmodernism has an "incredulity."
Another Marxist such as Fredric Jameson, for example, would resist
my position that postmodernism is historical. Jameson's consistent
references to postmodernism as superficial and depthless (see, for
example, "Postmodernism, Or the Cultural Logic of Late Capitalism") is based, I believe, on his own, traditional, Marxist view of
"genuine historicity." It is precisely the genuineness of *any* history
that postmodernism challenges, in addition to the depth/surface dichotomy as the standard for meaning and worth. As Hutcheon (1988)
states, postmodernism

> teaches and enacts the recognition of the fact that the
> social, historical, and existential "reality" of the past is
> *discursive* reality when it is used as the referent of art,
> and so the only "genuine historicity" becomes that
> which would openly acknowledge its own discursive,
> contingent identity. . . . [E]ven the most self-conscious
> and parodic of contemporary works do not try to escape,
> but indeed foreground, the historical, social, ideological
> contexts in which they have existed and continue to ex-
> ist. (24–25)

This is what Hal Foster (1983) refers to in terms of a "postmodernism
of resistance" which "seeks to question rather than exploit cultural
codes, to explore rather than conceal social and political affiliations"
(xii).

As a theory of resistance, postmodernism owes a great deal to
African-American and feminist theory and practice. Much of what
motivates these separate interrogations and many of the positions
taken in response to the marginalizing of the experience of people
of color and of women have provided an impetus to the political push
of the postmodern moment. More specifically, the theory and practice
of African-Americans and of feminists have highlighted a refocusing
on history, which I suggest is a first principle of the postmodern
moment. Questions of representation and of histories untold, or told
with a will to power, have been clarified and formulated with elegance
within ethnic theory and feminist theory. Such theories have also
brought to the fore the relationship between racial and/or gender
difference and questions of authority and power which are integral
to the postmodern moment. For example, when Hutcheon (1988)
speaks of how "the concept of alienated otherness (based on binary
oppositions that conceal hierarchies) gives way . . . to that of differences, that is to the assertion, not of centralized sameness, but of
decentered community" (12), we may think of Toni Morrison's communities (in *Sula* and *Song of Solomon*, for example). We are not
allowed to read or envision these communities as 'other'; that is, we
may not use the humanist subject as white and male as the measuring

stick against which all else is compared. Rather, we are introduced to differences and multiplicity within a particular community. When one Morrison character in *Song of Solomon*, Pilate, says of 'black': "There're five or six kinds of black. Some silky, some wooly. Some just empty. Some like fingers. And it don't stay still. It moves and changes from one kind of black to another. . . . May as well be a rainbow" (1977, 40), she is breaking through "the enclosure of negation" (Gates, 1984), the dynamic by which the terms of one's assertion are derived from a discourse determined not by self but by other.

This is not to say, however, that we may formulate a one-to-one relationship between postmodernism and African-American or feminist theory or practice. Nor do I mean to suggest a one-to-one relationship between African-American and feminist theory and practice, each of which might as well be a rainbow. Just as there is much feminism, for example, happening within a postmodern moment, there is much that is inconsistent with that moment, and this is, quite simply, because there is no such thing as one Feminism. Feminist discourse differs radically, depending on the positioning of the feminist speaking. There are feminists who consider themselves postmodernist. Feminists who consider themselves poststructuralist. And feminists who think that to speak in these terms is an act of political suicide. For example, 'cultural feminism'—"the ideology of a female nature or female essence reappropriated by feminists themselves in an effort to revalidate undervalued female attributes" (Alcoff, 1988, 408)—remains at odds with poststructuralist feminism, which holds that the cultural feminist response to sexism

> does not criticize the fundamental mechanism of oppressive power used to perpetuate sexism and in fact reinvokes that mechanism in its supposed solution. The mechanism of power referred to here is the construction of the subject by a discourse that weaves knowledge and power into a coercive structure that "forces the individual back on himself and ties him to his own identity in

a constraining way." (Alcoff, 1988, 415, quoting Foucault [1982, 781]; see Chapter 3)

These are just two positions within feminism, but the contestation
is clear, and the stakes are high.

The debates within feminism go a long way toward suggesting
why there are far fewer women than men writing postmodern fiction,
fiction which enacts a critique of the liberal humanist ideology of
representation and Identity. (Hutcheon's extensive bibliography of
theory and practice in *A Poetics of Postmodernism* [1988] lists over
150 novels, about 20 of which are by women.) Such a critique may
seem to some feminists like an odd direction to take in light of the
fact that for centuries identity and subjectivity were exactly what was
denied women. Thus, many feminists believe that to work outside
of an essentialist frame of reference is to allow the continued mar-
ginalization of woman-as-object. In response, however, poststructuralist feminists have asked:

> if feminist theory lets itself be guided by questions such
> as what is women's language, literature, style or expe-
> rience from where does it get its faith in the form of
> these questions to get at truth, if not from the same
> central store that supplies humanism with its faith in
> the universal truth of man? . . . If feminist theory can
> be content to propose cosmetic modifications on the face
> of humanism and its institutions, will it have done any-
> thing more than reproduce the structure of woman's ex-
> clusion in the same code which has been extended to
> include her? (Kamuf, 1982, 44–45)

A forceful argument, to be sure, but one that may sound empty to
someone who hesitates before a critique of subjectivity quite simply
because she has never been allowed the position of subject from which
to extend this critique.

One response by a feminist poststructuralist is to suggest that
while continuing to demystify structures of subjectivity, "feminist

historiography has to go 'beyond' by patiently accounting for different patterns of subject-formation" (Radhakrishnan, 1988, 196). Feminists, in other words, walk the fence. On one side is the slip into the essentialism of humanism, which 'naturally' privileges the subject-as-male, or encourages the feminist to reverse and repeat the binary trap; on the other side is a potential negation of the feminist claim to its own language or home, a politically dangerous stance. These questions are further complicated when considered within the framework of the African-American women's community, which often sees feminism as the domain of white women. Barbara Christian (1988) states:

> [S]eldom do feminist theorists take into account the complexity of life—that women are of many races and ethnic backgrounds with different histories and cultures and that as a rule women belong to different classes that have different concerns. (75)

Although these issues are far more complicated, and the debates more sophisticated, than may be dealt with within the scope of this Introduction, I believe that the postmodern moment provides a space within which these questions may be positively worked on. I do not say resolved; resolution and closure are not goals of the postmodern moment. Radhakrishnan (1988) presents the potential of the intersection of feminist historiography with poststructuralist thought, in which feminist historiography escapes the danger "of turning into a superficial reversal of forces of power" (189) by

> tapping on the one hand into the Utopian radicality of post-structuralist difference and alterity, and on the other, historicizing or semanticizing this very radicality by way of a here-and-now and a short-term program of affirmative transformation. (193)

Such a feminist historiography shares with postmodernism a counter-mnemonic project (see Chapters 5 and 6):

> As historiography, feminist theory is different precisely
> because it is still interested in creating and transforming
> history. . . . [F]eminist critical theory aligns historiogra-
> phy and critical theorizing with the making and doing
> of history. (Radhakrishnan, 1988, 202–03)

Coherent with the postmodern moment is the feminist concept
of 'identity politics' in which "one's identity is taken (and defined)
as a political point of departure, as a motivation for action, and as
a delineation of one's politics" (Alcoff, 1988, 431–32). Identity politics allows individuals to choose their identity as a member of one
or more groups as their political point of departure, with the recognition that such identity is "a *posit* that is politically paramount"
(emphasis mine). One recognizes "one's identity as always a construction yet also a necessary point of departure" (Alcoff, 1988, 432).
Nancy Fraser and Linda Nicholson would refer here to a "postmodern feminism" in which

> unitary notions of "woman" and "feminine gender iden-
> tity" [would be replaced] with plural and complexly con-
> structed conceptions of social identity, treating gender as
> one relevant strand among others, attending also to class,
> race, ethnicity, age, and sexual orientation. (1988, 101)

I say that the concept of identity politics is coherent with the postmodern moment because this moment is grounded in the historical,
the social, and the political, and highlights the potential of the local
and the limited, the multiple, and the provisional. Teresa de Lauretis
(1986, 14) sees this as "a shift, a development . . . in the feminist
understanding of female subjectivity":

> from the earlier view of woman defined purely by sexual
> difference (i.e., in relation to man) to the more difficult
> and complex notion that the female subject is a site of
> differences; differences that are not only sexual or only
> racial, economic, or (sub)cultural, but all of these to-

> gether, and often enough at odds with one another. These
> differences . . . remain concretely embedded in social and
> power relations. (14)

This emphasis on 'difference' is an example of how feminism, for
example, may speak within the postmodern moment.

Unfortunately, much of the theory within the postmodern moment has had a rather chilling effect, keeping many readers from
seeing its possibilities, specifically because of its often bewildering
terminology. Barbara Christian (1988) refers to the "race for theory"
and speculates that contemporary theory has within its program, if
not the intention, the result of silencing African-American women
critics in speaking of their "own" literature:

> [T]he new emphasis on literary critical theory is as heg-
> emonic as the world it attacks. I see the language it cre-
> ates as one that mystifies rather than clarifies our con-
> dition, making it possible for a few people who know
> that particular language to control the critical scene. (71)

Many of Christian's criticisms are apt, but much of her insistence on
how criticism must be done *is done* or is at least possible within the
postmodern moment. For example, she says we need to "remain open
to the intricacies of the intersection of language, class, race, and
gender in the literature" (69). This is a postmodern as well as an
African-American feminist assertion. Christian also refutes the notion of being identified as "somebody's *other*" (70), a notion also
refuted by postmodernism's emphasis on difference, rather than on
the Self/Other dichotomy. But Christian's most acute criticism is that
"when theory is not rooted in practice, it becomes prescriptive, exclusive, elitish" (74). She is right. One potential of the postmodern
moment could be a refusal to recognize the barriers between theory
and practice. For example, theory may become the "erotics of reading" (Roland Barthes's *The Pleasure of the Text*) and fiction may
become philosophy/theology (Umberto Eco's *The Name of the Rose*).

The second point I want to make in response to Christian's call for theory rooted in practice is the basis for the methodology of this text: although fiction and theory within the postmodern moment use widely varying narrative strategies, they share the same discursive space. That is, they are often saying the same thing about and within the postmodern moment. My project here is to present some of the theory and some of the fiction side by side, read together to help define the moment within which, and to which, they speak. The theory is not used to explicate the fiction. The fiction is not presented as proof of the theory. Neither theory nor fiction is presented as the site of Truth. My intent is not to interpret, but to use; read together, the fiction and theory indicate critiques and concerns of the moment. But Christian has good reason to fear an exclusionary propensity to contemporary theory. All too often, readers outside of a specific group of academics and intellectuals are not privy to the language used to discuss our culture. What does it mean to critique representation, to critique subjectivity, what is intertextuality, what is historiographic metafiction, structuralism, poststructuralism, *différance*, counter-memory, genealogy? This text is designed to make these crucial concepts available to a larger audience. Although the concepts presented here are just the bare bones, some isolated moments within the postmodern, this book is intended to open up a field of questions for the reader, so that s/he has some of the tools necessary to more readily understand postmodern debates and dialogues, be they in fiction, art, or theory. This text is not meant to replace the primary texts; it is an introduction.

Chapter 1 presents the Italo Calvino short story, "A Sign in Space," as a means of introducing the reader to the language of structuralism. The tenets of structuralism make possible the questions of poststructuralism, and both often take place within the postmodern moment. Chapter 2 introduces the critique of representation with the help of J.M. Coetzee's *Foe* and Jacques Derrida's essays, "Structure, Sign and Play in the Discourse of the Human Sciences" and "Différance." From structuralism's closure of the sign (the signi*fier* as that which represents the signi*fied*), we move to the poststructuralist deconstruction of the sign, in which each signifer's signified itself becomes a signifier in an endless chain of signification. Chapter 3 introduces the critique of subjectivity. Part I of this chapter includes an overview of the concept of the subject as an historically specific construct. In Part II I read Michel Foucault's essay "The Subject and Power" along with Michel Tournier's *Friday* to introduce, among other things, the relationship between subjectivity and power. In Chapter 4 I use Roland Barthes's essay "From Work to Text" in conjunction with *Foe* and *Friday* as a means of discussing intertextuality: the momentary compendium of that which has come before and is now; the space where 'meanings' intersect. Chapter 5 then brings the theoretical tools gathered thus far to the crucial discussion of history within the postmodern moment. The counter-memory of three novels (Christa Wolf's *Cassandra*, Timothy Findley's *Famous Last Words*, and Salman Rushdie's *Midnight's Children*), each an example of 'historiographic metafiction', is highlighted, along with Michel Foucault's essay, "Nietzsche, Genealogy, History."

Postmodernism resists closure, but a physical text must end. The last chapter (6) of this book ends with a series of questions that we must ask of ourselves as we learn to use the theoretical tools of the postmodern moment: What agendas power the use of these tools? When are the concerns of the postmodern—which I suggest make sense within a Euro(Anglo)centric tradition—inappropriate as interpretive strategies? How is the will to power that is lodged within postmodern interpretation displayed? I use Toni Morrison's *Beloved* as a vehicle through which to ask these, and other, questions.

The reader is cautioned that the choice of the fiction and the theory used here reflects a studied capriciousness. This introductory text could have been written using a completely different list of authors and works. For example, another person writing this book may have chosen to use an essay from Julia Kristeva instead of Roland Barthes to discuss intertextuality. This caveat is perhaps even more important when considering the fiction used. A novel such as Angela Carter's *The Infernal Desire Machines of Dr. Hoffman* could have been used to teach any one of the following chapters. Perhaps a text such as this could have been designed using solely works by people of color, for example. Or using solely works by Americans. I chose texts I know and enjoy.

One of the greatest dangers of a book such as this, which singles out specific texts as models of a sort, is its (undesired) valorization of the notion of a canon. Granted, I have chosen texts which I think merit reading, but I hope the reader will recognize throughout this book a refusal of the concept of certain texts as naturally 'representative' of postmodernism. These fictional texts, I propose, make a space for the interpretations which I have chosen to bring to bear. But there can be no doubt that my interpretations are a domination reflecting my own agenda.

Some final warnings. I encourage the reader to keep in mind that this text itself has decidedly anti-postmodern moments. The structure of this book suggests that there are five or so 'central' ideas to know about postmodernism and then it will all make sense, then the reader will know all about the postmodern moment. On the contrary, this is just the moment of entry into a full, contradictory, argumentative realm of discussion. Secondly, texts, especially texts that act as introductions, have the effect of concretizing concepts, as if they were non-negotiable and written in stone. This is precisely the type of thought that is incompatible with the postmodern moment. Because this is an introduction I have tried not to send readers in too many directions at one time. By resisting making multiple references to other related works and to the critiques of the theorists and their works and of the fiction writers and their works, I have taken the chance of inviting closure and of presenting a false sense of control over the material. But there is no closure, no absolute control. Each chapter is meant to provide access to vectors of discussion; as each question is clarified, the reader is encouraged to say, "Yeah, but . . ."

I

Structuralism and Italo Calvino's "A Sign in Space"

Fiction and theory in the postmodern moment emphasize the role of language as a constituent of reality. Not surprisingly, then, much of the criticism of the moment is at least conversant with linguistics. More specifically, it is often through a study of Ferdinand de Saussure's contributions to our understanding of linguistic semiotics (in his *Course in General Linguistics*) that we approach structuralism, and then, poststructuralism. I unpack some of these relationships in this chapter by reading Italo Calvino's short story "A Sign in Space" from *Cosmicomics* as an introduction to semiotics (the study of signs) and to a general methodology of structuralism. Although structuralism participates in a movement toward a postmodern logic in its critique of representation by way of its emphasis on meaning as relying on difference rather than on essence, ultimately, with its emphasis on closure, it resides outside the postmodern moment. In other words, although structuralist logic denies the empiricist world view privileged by our tradition of Western metaphysical philosophy, it does not engage in the 'play' or endless deferral of meaning that poststructuralism brings to the postmodern moment.

Structuralism most indicates a postmodern logic in its suggestion that meaning is based on relationships within a system, and is thus, social: we are defined by language, signs, structures. What I indicate as this book progresses are some of the social and political ramifications of these changing paradigms of meaning. Thus, although much of this chapter remains on the level of providing and explicating terminology, in later chapters, this terminology will be important in identifying the implications of, for example, the critique of representation or of subjectivity. In this spirit I introduce Saussurean concepts on a micro-level (in terms of linguistics) in this chapter in order to generalize these concepts for use on a macro-level (in terms of social relations) in later chapters.

In Calvino's *Cosmicomics* each story begins with a scientific 'truth', that is, an assertion based on a particular community's particular way of looking at the world at a particular time. In "A Sign in Space" that assertion is: *Situated in the external zone of the Milky Way, the Sun takes about two hundred million years to make a complete revolution of the Galaxy.*

Immediately, we note that the term "revolution" incorporates a series of traditional assumptions: it sets up the sense of closure—what goes around, comes around; and it implies that the circular pattern is determined by a center (that which defines, and thus provides, limits). Although the center (the Sun) is on the circumference, it is the position from which meaning (in this case, the determination of time) emanates. The concept of a center from which meaning emanates is logocentrism. Logocentrism is packed with meaning. The logos is not simply *a* word, but rather *the* word, that which comes before all else, that around which meaning must take place, the Law. As such, logocentrism refers to a guiding principle not just of written texts, and not just of human beings, but of the natural universe. It is precisely against this logocentrism that many contemporary critical theorists battle (through structuralism, and then through poststructuralism's simultaneous use and critique of structuralism). As Jacques Derrida, in "Structure, Sign and Play in the Discourse of the Human Sciences" (1978) states:

> Successively, and in a regulated fashion, the center receives different forms or names. The history of meta-

physics, like the history of the West, is the history of these metaphors and metonymies. Its matrix . . . is the determination of Being as *presence* in all senses of this word. It could be shown that all the names related to fundamentals, to principles, or to the center have always designated an invariable presence . . . (essence, existence, substance, subject) . . . transcendentality, consciousness, God, man, and so forth. (279–80)

The notion of an essential, invariable center, of logocentrism, is that presence from which meaning emanates. A critique of logocentrism, then, must include a rigorous examination of language because within the logocentrism of our Western tradition language provides the mediating system through which thought (or meaning) is physically manifested. And language is not an 'innocent' vehicle to express thought; rather, it molds thought into its own conceptual categories which replicate a logocentric pattern. A poststructuralist contribution toward our understanding of language is the realization that language relies on hierarchical oppositions—between presence and absence, reality and appearance, between inside and outside, between meaning and form—and that the first term takes priority, whereas the second is conceived in relation to the first, as derivative and dependent.

In terms of linguistics, there is assumed to be a prior reality or essence that can be represented through some form of signifier; that is, the signifier is a means of providing access to these essences or reality. This is essentially an Aristotelian theory of representation, based on the idea that language represents thought, which in turn represents the world. It is these logocentric, metaphysical assertions about our world and thus, our language, which structuralist thought attempts to undermine. Saussure questioned the basis of logocentrism by positing meaning as arbitrary and determined by 'difference' rather than as essential, invariable, self-identical. In linguistic terms, he did not accept the representational view of meaning as that which appeared naturally between the referent (the material thing) and the sign (that which points to or reflects the referent). Rather, Saussure separated the sign itself into the acoustical or graphic *signifier* (that which does the pointing) and the *signified* (the idea or concept to which the signifier points). In the process of fixing the site of meaning within this schema, a referent becomes unimportant. To suggest that meaning is not only arbitrary, but determined by difference, is to posit a general category of conceptual meaning that must be described in terms of its outside boundaries, rather than by its contents, but is still viewed, if temporarily, as a closed system. We will be able to see this view of meaning transpire within Calvino's story.

As I slowly present "A Sign in Space," I discuss changes in our thought about language, knowledge, world views. We should not view this movement as a linear, cause-and-effect progression, but rather as characterized by rupture, change, and chance. I do not suggest that we get closer to 'true' knowledge as time progresses; instead, my emphasis is on shifting paradigms of thought. In this story, we first see the character Qfwfq (I will call her/him/it 'Q') working within an empiricist framework, as evidenced by a positivist confidence in the representational connection between referent and signifier (i.e., without referents language is meaningless) and an assertion of the subject's control. 'Subject' in this context means the subject of experience, the 'I' that thinks, perceives, speaks. As the story progresses, Q's assumptions indicate a shift toward a structuralist paradigm, with its emphasis on meaning as arbitrary and determined by difference or relationships. This structuralist emphasis on difference then shifts into the inevitable play of poststructuralist *différance*. In linguistic terms, although poststructuralism adheres to structuralism's tenet that meaning is based on difference, it finds structuralism's concept of the sign—based on the distinction between the sensible and the intelligible, that is, the signifier and the signified— to be just one instance of a reliance on binary logic which continues the logocentric tradition (of basing a binary hierarchy on presence versus absence). Whereas structuralism separated even further the referent from the sign, the poststructuralists separate the signified from the signifier, speaking now of chains of signifiers (each signified becomes itself a signifier), and thus, open what had been a closed system of meaning. Poststructuralist *différance* (see Chapter 2) refers not only to the difference between signified and signifier (to differ), but more so, to the endless deferral of meaning as each signified becomes itself a signifier (to defer).

In short, I present "A Sign in Space" as an allegorical construction and deconstruction of Saussurean structuralism. But mine is certainly not an innocent, unbiased interpretation. In fact, this story, as well as my entire work here refutes the possibility of such an interpretation. Keep in mind that this text is dedicated to the process of reading (in the sense of opening up meanings), not of interpreting (in the sense of closing in on a particular meaning). This is a reading of a story simultaneous with a reading of some contemporary critical theory.

Right, that's how long it takes, not a day less,—Qfwfq said,—once, as I went past, I drew a sign at a point in space, just so I could find it again two hundred million years later, when we went by the next time around.

Our first thought here may be that Q decides to make a sign in order to tell time, but that's not the case: Q already knows (somehow) that the revolution takes 200 million years. Our first task, then, is to define 'sign' as presented in this context. It is, first, something that is created, and thus, controlled, by the subject, and its purpose appears to be communication and thus language, but only with Q himself: he makes the sign "just so I could find it again." As such, the sign performs as a mirror, as that thing created by a subject which reflects and represents the subject. The sign is, at this point, a symbol or icon; that is, it is a fusion of content and form. When Q draws a sign which acts as a mirror, content and form are identical. His sign is a unitary thing.

What sort of sign? It's hard to explain because if I say sign to you, you immediately think of a something that can be distinguished from a something else, but nothing could be distinguished from anything there; you immediately think of a sign made with some implement or with your hands, and then when you take the implement or your hands away, the sign remains, but in those days there were no implements or even hands, or teeth, or noses, all things that came along afterwards, a long time afterwards. As to the form a sign should have, you say it's no problem because, what-

ever form it may be given, a sign only has to serve as a sign, that is, be different or else the same as other signs: here again it's easy for you young ones to talk, but in that period I didn't have any examples to follow, I couldn't say I'll make it the same or I'll make it different, there were no things to copy, nobody knew what a line was, straight or curved, or even a dot, or a protuberance or a cavity.

Q's point is well taken. If we are thinking in structuralist terms, we can't yet think Q's sign. Q posits his sign as pure essence. For Saussure, however, objects are defined by their relations with other objects and not by essences of some kind. Saussure states that

> the ultimate law of language is, dare we say, that nothing can ever reside in a single term. This is a direct consequence of the fact that linguistic signs are unrelated to what they designate, and that therefore *a* cannot designate anything without the aid of *b* and vice versa, or, in other words, that both have value only by the differences between them, or that neither has value, in any of its constituents, except through this same network of forever negative differences. (in Culler, 1977, 64)

Saussure would say that we can never think an 'original' sign: since meaning is determined by difference, every sign has to have something that is different from it in order to come to be, in order to make sense. So with sign as difference (which presupposes other items within the system for comparison), we seem to be unable to conceptualize Q's sign at all. Unless, of course, we think of the difference between sign and space. Q suggests, in fact, what our understanding of the sign will become: that which has meaning because of difference, "something that can be distinguished from something else." But already we have moved ahead (as Q suggests) into a later paradigm of thought. In this and the following passage we see that Q positions his sign more comfortably within traditional metaphysical thought, with the sign still as symbol, where referent and sign are unitary. *I conceived the idea of making a sign, that's true enough, or rather, I conceived the idea of considering a sign a something that I felt*

like making, so when, at that point in space and not in another, I
made something, meaning to make a sign, it turned out that I really
had made a sign, after all.

In other words, considering it was the first sign ever made in
the universe, or at least in the circuit of the Milky Way, I must
admit it came out very well.

While we could allow Q this moment of glory, we must also be
allowed to question, as must he: what makes him think it's the only
sign? Where did the notion of sign come from? Still, his pleasure has
a familiar ring to it as we hear the echo of God's pleasure in his
creation, "And He saw it was good." First sign, The Word. In this
replication of God's creation, thought and becoming are simultaneous. This is the basis, ultimately, of the ontology of Western logocentrism. God is the Word and the creator of the Word. Q thinks
a sign, the thought and sign are simultaneous, and it was good.

Thus, we have the situation of the subject who, in his actions,
becomes the center which determines meaning by creating a sign.
Within this logic exists the possibility of the origin as something
that dwells within and emanates from the subject. As well as the
subject as creator of meaning, the sense of meaning here is that which
is immanent with the sign. Intent and being, content and form, are
inseparable; the sign consists of a referent (what something is, what
can be pointed to) and the sign (that which refers to the referent,
that which does the pointing). The referent and the sign—the latter
of which in structuralist terms will become signified and signifier—
cannot be thought separately because the sign represents exactly the
referent. The ontology of Western metaphysics, and the basis for
humanism, is intact at this point in the story: Q is the subject creating
meaning and meaning is immanent in Q's sign.

Visible? What a question! Who had eyes to see with in those days?
Nothing had ever been seen by anything, the question never even
arose. Recognizable, yes, beyond any possibility of error: because
all the other points in space were the same, indistinguishable, and
instead, this one had the sign on it.

Q's sign has 'value' or meaning because of its place within the
(solar) system: it is *not* what everything else *is*. In Saussure's words:

> concepts are purely differential, not positively defined by
> their content but negatively defined by their relations
> with other terms of the system. Their most precise char-
> acteristic is that they are what the others are not. (in
> Culler, 1977, 36)

Q, however, looks at the sign in terms of a Western metaphysical
sense of representation: he intended to make a sign, and having intended to do so, he did; the sign is the representation of his intent
and the meaning is mirrored by the form.

So as the planets continued their revolutions, and the solar
system went on in its own, I soon left the sign far behind me,
separated from it by the endless fields of space. And I couldn't help
thinking about when I would come back and encounter it again,
and how I would know it, and how happy it would make me, in
that anonymous expanse, after I had spent a hundred thousand
light-years without meeting anything familiar, nothing for hundreds
of centuries, for thousands of millennia; I'd come back and there
it would be in its place, just as I had left it, simple and bare, but
with that unmistakable imprint, so to speak, that I had given it.

Q's delight is that of the acting subject who is responsible for
language, "that unmistakable imprint," which represents him.
Through ownership Q is able to recover and secure the sign's meaning
from that which is 'different' into that which is 'familiar', or same.
With the word "imprint" Q suggests that his sign is, to him, a material referent. But with Q's remove from his sign, we may begin to
think of the terms signified and signifier as a definition of sign: the
signifier as the "imprint," the form which signifies, and the signified
as the concept indicated. In this case, the idea signified is that moment
of familiarity to which Q wants to return. In structuralist terms, the
referent needn't be thought (or present) at all for the sign proper to
be understood.

The relationship between that concept of sign (as signified) which
Q remembers and the 'graphic' sign (signifier) by which Q tries to
remember the signified, brings to the fore the first principle of Saussure's theory of language: the linguistic sign is arbitrary. Any com-

bination of signifier and signified is an arbitrary entity. In our story, for example, we do not even know the form of the "imprint" Q has left behind; clearly the form itself has no direct representational bearing on the concept of sign that Q intended. This arbitrariness goes hand-in-glove with the definition of meaning or value as difference. That the relationship between signifier and signified is arbitrary suggests that we need to think outside the realm of fixed or absolute universal concepts. Nevertheless, Q still sees his sign as 'fixed'.

Slowly the Milky Way revolved, with its fringe of constellations and planets and clouds, and the Sun along with the rest, toward the edge. In all that circling, only the sign remained still, in an ordinary spot, out of all the orbit's reach (to make it, I had leaned over the border of the Galaxy a little, so it would remain outside and all those revolving worlds wouldn't crash into it), in an ordinary point that was no longer ordinary since it was the only point that was surely there, and which could be used as a reference point to distinguish other points.

I thought about it day and night; in fact, I couldn't think about anything else; actually, this was the first opportunity I had had to think something; or I should say: to think something had never been possible, first because there were no things to think about, and second because signs to think of them by were lacking, but from the moment there was that sign, it was possible for someone thinking to think of a sign, and therefore that one, in the sense that the sign was the thing you could think about and also the sign of the thing thought, namely, itself.

As our story progresses, it's increasingly necessary to give dual interpretations to Q's 'sign'. On the one hand, thought and sign are still simultaneous ("the sign was the thing you could think about and also the sign of the thing thought"). On the other hand, we see Q's sign as separating into "things to think about" (the concept: signified) and into something to "think of [things] by" (the graphic or spoken pointer: signifier). In the traditional empiricist mode, the thing thought about is the material referent and the thing to think of the referent by is the sign. For the structuralist, the idea or concept is the thing thought about (the signified) and the thing to think the signified by is the signifier. This distinction between the signified and the referent is crucial, for, in fact, there is no need to discuss the referent at all within Saussure's system. It is the (arbitrary) relationship between signifier and signified in language which encapsulates meaning. When meaning is defined as difference, the referent is replaced by the signified. What is needed for meaning is the concept or idea or possibility of the thing rather than the thing itself.

So the situation was this: the sign served to mark a place but at the same time it meant that in that place there was a sign (something far more important because there were plenty of places but there was only one sign) and also at the same time that sign was mine, the sign of me, because it was the only sign I had ever made and I was the only one who had ever made signs. It was like a name, the name of that point, and also my name that I had signed on that spot; in short, it was the only name available for everything that required a name.

Q again provides a Saussurean definition of sign as signified and signifier: "that which marks a place" is the signifier, and "that place" is the signified. In structuralist terms they are thought separately, but do not exist independently of each other. As Q states, they are "at the same time." That Q is not thinking in structuralist terms, however, is clear in Q's boast of ownership of, and identification with, the sign: "that sign was mine, the sign of me." In Q's universe at this point, the subject gives meaning to language, replicating the Aristotelian view of language as a representation of ideas in the soul or mind. Still, Q seems to suggest that the sign (and thus language) identifies the subject. Now, in a sense, these views are ontological worlds apart. In Western metaphysics the subject is a center which gives meaning, but in structuralism, the subject is defined and placed culturally and historically. In a moment we will look at the vocabulary of language in terms of community and individual, which we will need in order to speak of the subject as defined by language. For the time being, however, with one foot in the realm of logocentrism, we'll look at Q's association of the sign with name.

Q invites a dialogue about the position of the Proper Name in language when he says that his sign is "like a name, the name of that point, and also my name ... it was the only name available for everything that required a name." By positing a simultaneity between "the name of that point, and also my name," Q reinforces the empiricist, metaphysical stance which allows a direct connection between signifier and referent. The proper name doesn't work by way of a concept, that is, by way of a signified. Instead, the proper name functions as a symbol. This realm of the proper name, and thus, the moment in which Q is located at this point in his story, is the realm of representational purity, where the referent and the sign (as signifier) are one.[1]

Transported by the sides of the Galaxy, our world went navigating through distant spaces, and the sign stayed where I had left it to mark that spot, and at the same time it marked me, I carried it with me, it inhabited me, possessed me entirely, came between me and everything with which I might have attempted to establish a relationship.

Q's sign is still perceived as stable. Not mixed up with time, it is some pure essence. And that "it marked me ... inhabited me" again indicates that the subject and the sign of the subject coincide, as with the proper name. But when Q introduces the word "relationship," the "sign" slips toward structuralist terminology, because it introduces the sense of a language shared within a community, and places an emphasis on meaning as social. The phrase: "[it] came between me and everything with which I might have attempted to establish a relationship" suggests a Saussurean definition of *langue*— that system that precedes, that dictates, that structures, that provides the form for language, and, by extension, for relationships within a community. Saussure states, *langue* "is the social side of speech, outside the individual who can never create or modify it by himself; it exists only by virtue of a sort of contract signed by the members of the community" (in Harland, 1987, 12).

We have already learned that Saussure, in defining the units of language, distinguished between the purely relational and abstract units (the signifieds) and their material realizations (the referents). Saussure then sets up the distinction between *langue* and *parole*:

> la langue is the system of a language, the language as a
> system of forms, whereas parole is actual speech, the
> speech acts that are made possible by the language. (in
> Culler, 1977, 39)

The distinction Saussure makes in separating *langue* from *parole* is
to separate what is social from what is individual, or, in Saussure's
words, "what is essential from what is ancillary or accidental" (in
Culler, 1977, 4). Saussure's construction here, while seemingly based
on a logocentric hierarchy of presence/absence or "essential"/"accidental," has the effect of turning the logocentric (representational)
universe on its head. This is the case because he posits social meanings (in the form of language categories/*langue*) as prior to objective
things. In other words, there is a system which is always present
(although perhaps not available to immediate consciousness), and
always at work structuring behavior. Such a concept has aspects that
are coherent within the postmodern moment and aspects that are
antithetical to the postmodern moment. Coherent with postmodern
logic is the emphasis placed here on meaning as social or collective.
Such an emphasis begins to free meaning from absolute representation and to move it toward the postmodern notion of meaning as
constructed. Individual experience is understood in social terms. But
the structuralist paradigm closes this movement down just as it opens
it up, by referring to social actions as a system of norms. Thus, the
absoluteness of one-to-one representation is replaced by the absoluteness of rules and mechanisms (for Saussure, the rules of a language). It remains for poststructuralist theory to historicize these
rules, and thus, to break open the closed structural system. This move
by poststructuralism, however, would have been unthinkable without
structuralism's rupture of meaning, from pure essence to social construction.

In terms of our story what is turned on its head is the idea of
Q (temporarily representative of logocentric 'man') as that being
which creates and defines language. The alternative presented is of
Q as defined by language, by signs, by structures. Keep in mind this
sense of meaning as social, as derived from relationships, as Q's sign

changes from something that has meaning because Q, the subject, gave it meaning, to something that gives meaning to Q and Q's community.

As I waited to come back and meet it again, I could try to derive other signs from it and combinations of signs, series of similar signs and contrasts of different signs. But already tens and tens of thousands of millennia had gone by since the moment when I had made it (rather, since the few seconds in which I had scrawled it down in the constant movement of the Milky Way) and now, just when I needed to bear in mind its every detail (the slightest uncertainty about its form made uncertain the possible distinctions between it and other signs I might make), I realized that, though I recalled its general outline, its over-all appearance, still something about it eluded me, I mean if I tried to break it down into its various elements, I couldn't remember whether, between one part and the other, it went like this or like that. I needed it there in front of me, to study, to consult,

If Q's sign were synonymous with some pure essence, it would be unchangeable—he would not need to keep it in front of him to know its meaning. It would be what it is, and unable to alter in any way. But Q is recognizing what Saussure would say is the first rule of language: its arbitrariness. And once and for all, Q can no longer try to view the sign as referent/signifier, where the referent is "there in front of me, to study, to consult," unchanging, but must now view the sign as signified/signifier. As Q remembers the sign, he remembers an idea about the thing (the signified), and the signifier by which he attempts to remember that concept has only an arbitrary link to it.

Q's concern with the instability and changeability of his sign also allows us to look at the nature of the sign synchronically and diachronically. The diachronic study of language is the study of its evolution in time. The synchronic study of language is the study of the linguistic system in a particular state, without reference to time. Culler (1977) explains the notions of synchrony and diachrony in terms of the arbitrary nature of the sign:

> The fact that the sign is arbitrary or wholly contingent makes it subject to history but also means that signs require an ahistorical analysis. . . . Since the sign has no necessary core that must persist, it must be defined as a relational entity, in its relations to other signs. And the relevant relations are those which obtain at a particular time. (46)

In short, although structuralism highlights the synchronic, it also recognizes the influence of history on signs. This distinction between synchronic and diachronic analysis is not a case of 'either/or' or of a right or wrong way to look at language. Neither term negates the other. The terms exist simultaneously; whether something is looked at synchronically or diachronically depends on their use-value in light of a particular agenda. In fact, these terms reflect a moment in the structuralist paradigm which is full of tension. Structuralist semiotics and questions of history are not easily resolved: structuralism can be ahistorical or may be articulated historically. For example, a synchronic analysis assumes a hypothesized moment of stasis within a diachronic system (one that changes with time). It is thus a methodological fiction. On the surface we may want to make the connection between a synchronic analysis (with its emphasis on stasis) as the moment in structuralism which is outside the postmodern moment, and a diachronic analysis (with its emphasis on history and change) as within the postmodern moment. But things are not as simple as that. Structuralism's diachronic analysis assumes a linear, if not predictable, history. And that, as we shall see, is definitely not postmodern. Q 'waits' to 'catch up' with his sign so he can perform a synchronic analysis.

[B]ut instead it was still far away, I didn't yet know how far, because I had made it precisely in order to know the time it would take me to see it again, and until I had found it once more, I wouldn't know. Now, however, it wasn't my motive in making it that mattered to me, but how it was made, and I started inventing hypotheses about this how, and theories according to which a certain sign had to be perforce in a certain way, or else, proceeding by

exclusion, I tried to eliminate all the less probable types of sign to arrive at the right one, but all these imaginary signs vanished inevitably because that first sign was missing as a term of comparison.

It's a good thing that motive doesn't matter to Q, for he tells us at the beginning of the story that he made the sign "just so I could find it again two hundred million years later," and now he says he made the sign to act as a galactic clock. His perception of his motive is as unstable as his memory of the sign itself. That this "first sign" be "missing" is necessary by the very terms of structural linguistics. Since it is the nature of the sign to depend on difference, there can be no first sign found—each sign is what it is because it is not what other signs are. Yet Q is still evidencing patterns of thought consistent with Western metaphysics in that he posits his particular moment (in time and space) as a center from which he can look back and deduce what has come before, with his hypotheses and theories, to the point of relocating the 'origin'. Still caught within logocentric logic, he assumes that there is a 'truth' coincident with, and made intelligible by, the 'origin'.

As I racked my brain like this (while the Galaxy went on turning wakefully in its bed of soft emptiness and the atoms burned and radiated) I realized I had lost by now even that confused notion of my sign, and I succeeded in conceiving only interchangeable fragments of signs, that is, smaller signs within the large one, and every change of these signs-within-the-sign changed the sign itself into a completely different one; in short, I had completely forgotten what my sign was like and, try as I might, it wouldn't come back to my mind.

Here we have a clear presentation of synchrony within a diachronic process. When Q says that "every change of these signs-within-the-sign changed the sign itself into a completely different one," he reminds us of how each change in the system on a diachronic level alters the system itself, that is, the formal relationships of the signs within the system. The system itself, however, though changeable, is complete at each synchronic moment. Saussure's most famous example is of the chess game. Alan Thiher (1984) explains the analogy:

In likening historical change and fixed states to the moves in a chess match, Saussure claims that any given move in the game brings about a new fixed state that corresponds to the synchronic system at any given moment. After each diachronic change, after each move, the respective value of each piece in the game, or linguistic system, depends on the position of the piece on the board, much as in language each entity has value through its differential relation opposing it to all other terms in the system. And as in language each fixed moment is only temporary; subsequent moves are inevitable. . . . Meaning or value is determined by a relation within the game space of language itself, not by some relation to an exterior realm. (78–79)

That is what is meant when we say that structuralists view each moment as, in a sense, complete. Fredric Jameson (1972) explains,

Saussure's originality was to have insisted on the fact that language as a total system is complete at every moment, no matter what happens to have been altered in it a moment before. This is to say that the temporal model proposed by Saussure is that of a series of complete systems succeeding each other in time; that language is for him a perpetual present, with all the possibilities of meaning implicit in its every moment. . . . Saussure's is in a sense an existential perception: no one denies the *fact* of the diachronic, that sounds have their own history and that meanings change. Only for the speaker, at any moment in the history of the language, one meaning alone exists, the current one . . . (5)

This is not to say that structuralism is ahistorical. Saussure specifically states that "at every moment a language implies an established system and an evolution; at every moment it is a present institution and a product of the past" (in Culler, 1977, 100). The history of individual elements results in forms that the system uses, and for structuralism, the study of those systemic uses is the goal or purpose. But Q's notion of time is here definitely not structuralist. His emphasis is on meaning as synonymous with origin, not with the present.

Did I despair? No, this forgetfulness was annoying, but not irreparable. Whatever happened, I knew the sign was there waiting for me, quiet and still. I would arrive, I would find it again, and I would then be able to pick up the thread of my meditations. At a rough guess, I calculated we had completed half of our galactic revolution: I had only to be patient, the second half always seemed to go by more quickly. Now I just had to remember the sign existed and I would pass it again.

Day followed day, and then I knew I must be near. I was furiously impatient because I might encounter the sign at any moment. It's here, no, a little farther on, now I'll count up to a hundred ... Had it disappeared? Had we already gone past it? I didn't know. My sign had perhaps remained who knows where, behind, completely remote from the revolutionary orbit of our system. I hadn't calculated the oscillations to which, especially in those days, the celestial bodies' fields of gravity were subject, and which caused them to trace irregular orbits, cut like the flower of a dahlia. For about a hundred millennia I tormented myself, going over my calculations: it turned out that our course touched that spot not every galactic year but only every three, that is, every six hundred million solar years. When you've waited two hundred million years, you can also wait six hundred; and I waited; the way was long but I wasn't on foot, after all; astride the Galaxy I traveled through the light-years, galloping over the planetary and stellar orbits as if I were on a horse whose shoes struck sparks; I was in a state of mounting excitement; I felt I was going forth to conquer the only thing that mattered to me, sign and dominion and name ...

The irony is that Q has been unknowingly defining his sign in structuralist terms, and thus has called into question the logocentric notion of 'man' as 'he' who is in control of meaning; nonetheless, Q remains unaware of his own critique of subjectivity. After so many examples of not being in control of the sign, and thus, of language, he can still use the word "conquer." He believes in himself as the subject with the power to create meaning. From what we've learned of language thus far, we know before Q what to expect of his sign, and thus, his "dominion and name" before he gets back to where he thinks he first was.

I made the second circuit, the third. I was there. I let out a yell. At a point which had to be that very point, in the place of my sign, there was a shapeless scratch, a bruised, chipped abrasion of space. I had lost everything: the sign, the point, the thing that caused me—being the one who had made the sign at that point— to be me.

With the tampering of the sign, Q's dreams of its purity and unchangeability are shown to have been only dreams; Q's role as the subject who creates is lost. If his identity or subjectivity is based on "being the one who had made the sign," then the transiency of that sign negates his "dominion and name." This moment is a potent introduction to the critique of subjectivity in structuralism, in which sense is determined in terms of systems of signs, and not by tracing an event to a subject-as-source. In short, the structuralist enterprise often consists of explaining meanings in terms of structures or systems of convention which escape the subject's conscious grasp.

Space, without a sign, was once again a chasm, the void, without beginning or end, nauseating, in which everything—including me— was lost. (And don't come telling me that, to fix a point, my sign and the erasure of my sign amounted to the same thing; the erasure was the negation of the sign, and therefore didn't serve to distinguish one point from the preceding and successive points.)

But, of course, by this time the sign and the erasure are, if not the same thing, then at least, both signs. The erasure has meaning precisely because it is not the sign, just as the other signs Q has thought of have meaning because they are not Q's sign. Earlier, when Q says that "meaning to make a sign, it turned out that I really had made a sign after all," Q suggests the relationship between sign and agency. This relationship between sign and use of the sign is reintroduced through Q's crestfallen response to the (erased) sign. That is to say, Q's response indicates that the (erased) sign *did* "distinguish one point from the preceding and successive points." Q's disheartened reaction is that of the subject who loses his belief in his transcendent power of creation. Instead of the subject who controls, we have the agent who uses. The erasure of the sign indicates that it has no transcendental status; rather, it functions as a tool to be manipulated by an agent. To refer to agency is not to reintroduce the subject through the back door; rather, the notion of agency is consistent with the postmodern strategy of local and provisional intervention within particular systems. The notion of another 'agent' who could 'use' Q's sign, however, obviously had not occurred to Q.

I was disheartened and for many light-years I let myself be dragged along as if I were unconscious. When I finally raised my eyes (in the meanwhile, sight had begun in our world, and as a result, also life), I saw what I would never have expected to see. I saw it, the sign, but not that one, a similar sign, a sign unquestionably copied from mine, but one I realized immediately couldn't be mine, it was so squat and careless and clumsily pretentious, a wretched counterfeit of what I had meant to indicate with that sign whose ineffable purity I could only now—through contrast— recapture.

Structuralism's critique of logocentrism tells us that a 'first' sign just cannot be. It is the nature of all signs to be arbitrary, and thus recognized by their difference: a sign has meaning because it is what others are not. For Q the 'first' sign (or 'one' sign) means purity, not surprisingly more so because he can't recover it, but which he can only "recapture" through contrast. The second sign, (or 'another' sign) the "wretched counterfeit of what I had meant to indicate with that sign" takes on meaning because it isn't the first sign.

Who had played this trick on me? I couldn't figure it out. Finally, a plurimillennial chain of deductions led me to the solution: on another planetary system which performed its galactic revolution before us, there was a certain Kgwgk (the name I deduced afterwards, in the later era of names), a spiteful type, consumed with envy, who had erased my sign in a vandalistic impulse and then, with vulgar artifice, had attempted to make another.

It was clear that his sign had nothing to mark except Kgwgk's intention to imitate my sign, which was beyond all comparison. But at that moment the determination not to let my rival get the better of me was stronger than any other desire: I wanted immediately to make a new sign in space, a real sign that would make Kgwgk die of envy.

Q's thoughts at this point are full of blindnesses. He speaks of a "later era of names" when he has already identified that "first" pure sign with the name—that moment when referent and signifier are joined in a position of power. He says that Kgwgk "had attempted to make another [sign]," but his own act of recognition acknowledges that this was not merely an attempt; it was a success. Most ironic is his statement that his sign "was beyond all comparison." Quite the contrary, it was that which invited comparison, and which took on a different meaning with that comparison.

About seven hundred millions of years had gone by since I had first tried to make a sign, but I fell to work with a will. Now things were different, however, because the world, as I mentioned, was beginning to produce an image of itself, and in everything a form was beginning to correspond to a function, and the forms of that time, we believed, had a long future ahead of them (instead, we were wrong: take—to give you a fairly recent example—the dinosaurs), and therefore in this new sign of mine you could perceive the influence of our new way of looking at things, call it style if you like, that special way that everything had to be, there, in a certain fashion. I must say I was truly satisfied with it, and I no longer regretted that first sign that had been erased, because this one seemed vastly more beautiful to me.

But in the duration of that galactic year we already began to realize that the world's forms had been temporary up until then, and that they would change, one by one. And this awareness was accompanied by a certain annoyance with the old images, so that even their memory was intolerable. I began to be tormented by a thought: I had left that sign in space, that sign which had seemed so beautiful and original to me and so suited to its function, and which now, in my memory, seemed inappropriate, in all its pre-

tension, a sign chiefly of an antiquated way of conceiving signs and of my foolish acceptance of an order of things I ought to have been wise enough to break away from in time. In other words, I was ashamed of that sign which went on through the centuries, being passed by worlds in flight, making a ridiculous spectacle of itself and of me and of that temporary way we had had of seeing things. I blushed when I remembered it (and I remembered it constantly), blushes that lasted whole geological eras: to hide my shame I crawled into the craters of the volcanoes, in remorse I sank my teeth into the caps of the glaciations that covered the continents. I was tortured by the thought that Kgwgk, always preceding me in the circumnavigation of the Milky Way, would see the sign before I could erase it, and boor that he was, he would mock me and make fun of me, contemptuously repeating the sign in rough caricatures in every corner of the circumgalactic sphere.

Instead, this time the complicated astral timekeeping was in my favor. Kgwgk's constellation didn't encounter the sign, whereas our solar system turned up there punctually at the end of the first revolution, so close that I was able to erase the whole thing with the greatest care.

Q has been forced to look at history. He no longer thinks of his signs as having some ineffable purity; in fact, although his statement that "form was beginning to correspond to a function" replicates an empiricist mode of thought, at the same time he recognizes that a mode of thought, a "way of looking at things," can be described in terms of "style . . . that special way that everything had to be, there, in a certain fashion." The greatest change in Q's mindset is a tardy recognition of the temporality of "the world's forms," and that things "would change." Nonetheless, this recognition of historicity doesn't make Q look forward in anticipation of change, but rather, backward, in annoyance at what had been: he places himself on the continuum of time as that moment or position (the center, if not the origin) from which to make sense of what has gone before.

As Q talks about the changeableness of forms, of signs, we think about the changeableness of language, of systems, of structures, which in turn, alter what we 'know' within those systems. So when

Q talks about "style," we can think of the structuralist recognition of meaning (the sign) as being determined by historical and cultural structures. Q's chagrin has to do with the inevitability of change, and thus, the inability of any particular pattern of thought or of being to remain stable or knowable (or more distressing to Q, the impossibility of knowing just what the next "style" will bring). In relation to Q's chagrin we can look at the structural anthropologist Lévi-Strauss's (1966) discussion of particular systems of thought that provide meaning in prior cultures:

> when one takes account of the wealth and diversity of the raw material, only a few of the innumerable possible elements of which are made use of in the system, there can be no doubt that a considerable number of other systems of the same type would have been equally coherent and that no one of them is predestined to be chosen by all societies and all civilizations. The terms never have any intrinsic significance. Their meaning is one of "position"—a function of the history and cultural context on the one hand and of the structural system in which they are called upon to appear on the other. (55)

Meaning in this passage is bi-directional (but always positional): it is "a function of the history and cultural context" in that this context determines what goes into the system; and it is a function of the structural system itself. In short, systems of meaning are made up of arbitrary components and those components, or terms, take on meaning within the system depending on their position or relationships with other terms. Q's recognition of the changing "order of things" suggests that Q is not so far from being able to think within a synchronic moment to gain understanding.

What Q doesn't recognize, however, is that this 'moment' is a fiction, and that change cannot be arrested. Perhaps another way of looking at this particular blindness is to say that Q does not recognize another aspect of the concept of 'system': that position within the system determines meaning. As Jameson (1972) puts it, "you can see only as much as your model permits you to see; . . . the meth-odological starting point does more than simply reveal, it actually creates, the object of study" (14). And finally, we see that Q hasn't learned anything about the ineffectiveness of erasures in eradicating signs; that, the erasures themselves become signs.

Now, there wasn't a single sign of mine in space. I could start drawing another, but I knew that signs also allow others to judge the one who makes them, and that in the course of a galactic year tastes and ideas have time to change, and the way of regarding the earlier ones depends on what comes afterwards; in short, I was afraid a sign that now might seem perfect to me, in two hundred or six hundred million years would make me look absurd. Instead, in my nostalgia, the first sign, brutally rubbed out by Kgwgk, re-mained beyond the attacks of time and its changes, the sign created before the beginning of forms, which was to contain something that would have survived all forms, namely the fact of being a sign and nothing else.

Making signs that weren't that sign no longer held any interest for me; and I had forgotten that sign now, billions of years before. So, unable to make true signs, but wanting somehow to annoy Kgwgk, I started making false signs, notches in space, holes, stains, little tricks that only an incompetent creature like Kgwgk could mistake for signs.

Q's memory of that "first sign" is an obvious nostalgia for a dream of power. It's the nostalgia for the origin, the transcendental signified, the logos that is pure in its remove from change. Pure only in its unattainability, Q's sign is privileged precisely because it is irrecoverable. Q's terminology of "true" and "false" signs highlights the relation between the original and the highly valued. To Q, what comes first is "true," and those signs that follow, are "false." (See Chapter 5 for more discussion of the privileging of the origin as the site of Truth in history.) As discussed earlier, however, truth and falsity don't apply. What matters is relationship: content and meaning are no longer synonymous with 'essence', but rather with structure—content is form. Q's "true" and "false" signs are all signs. It is their difference, as Q sees it, that gives them meaning. Truth-value isn't the point any longer; use-value is. The signs have become a means of communication between Q and Kgwgk.

And still he furiously got rid of them with his erasings (as I could see in later revolutions), with a determination that must have cost him much effort. (Now I scattered these false signs liberally through space, to see how far his simple-mindedness would go.)

Observing these erasures, one circuit after the next (the Galaxy's revolutions had now become for me a slow, boring voyage without goal or expectation), I realized something: as the galactic years passed the erasures tended to fade in space, and beneath them what I had drawn at those points, my false signs—as I called them— began to reappear. This discovery, far from displeasing me, filled me with new hope. If Kgwgk's erasures were erased, the first he had made, there at that point, must have disappeared by now, and my sign must have returned to its pristine visibility!

Although Q contradicts himself, saying that his "first" sign may have "returned to its pristine visibility," when he told us earlier that it couldn't be defined by sight, Q here provides us with an image of intertextuality, a concept implied by structuralism, and given full play in poststructuralist theory (see Chapter 4). Intertextuality refers to the notion that all 'writing', all 'texts', are penetrated by and composed of traces of previous 'texts'. Each text must consist of a network of intersecting (known or recognizable) texts; otherwise it would have no meaning. Intertextuality is a postmodern concept in the sense that it denies the word (or the text) transcendental, representative status. Instead of representing some exact thing, idea, presence, the word (text) is the conditional moment which indicates all the words (texts) that have gone into making it understandable, approachable, meaningful.

The concept of intertextuality is situated within a system of meaning based on identity and difference. Within a semiotic system, signs do not remain fixed: a given form will not always have the same meaning wherever it appears. The meaning will be determined by the particular system or structure that provides the boundaries for that sign. In terms of literary works, intertextuality is a factor as works draw upon signs which exist prior to them, combining signs and drawing from them new meaning. In our story, Q's "false" signs (signs nonetheless) are made into new, different signs by Kgwgk's process of erasure. This is one moment of intertextuality: Kgwgk's signs draw upon previous existing signs. That Kgwgk's "erasures tended to fade in space," allowing Q's "false" signs to reappear, indicates that prior signs are always inherent in the present, even if not immediately identifiable.

We may also use Q's signs and Kgwgk's erasures as the opportunity to look at what is ultimately the totalizing logic of structuralism's scientific agenda: binarism. By 'totalizing' I refer to a particular logic dedicated to closure, in the sense that it presents an overarching framework according to which all the parts of the system are given a fixed meaning. Structuralism's binary logic is based on the primary distinction between identity and difference. This oppositional binarism is expressed in the nuts and bolts of structuralist logic: for example, in the distinctions between signifier and signified, *langue* and *parole*, synchrony and diachrony. These binary terms are thought of on both a micro- and macro-level. On the micro-level, for example, the structural linguist may refer to the binary opposition between distinctive features of the sound of consonants: 'diffuse' or 'compact'. For our purposes, however, it is most important to recognize the macro-level of binary oppositions. That is, the semiotics of structuralism in general allow for the abstracting of these very specific concepts from the micro-level of linguistics toward a consideration of macro-level (social) systems. As Culler (1981) explains, through semiotics

> we come to think of our social and cultural world as a series of sign systems, comparable with languages. What we live among and relate to are not physical objects and events; they are objects and events with meaning. . . . The point is that semiotics enables us to perceive in recent intellectual activity a general tendency, variously stated and of differing degrees of explicitness, to stress the role of symbolic systems in human experience and

thus to think in terms not of autonomous objects but of systems of relations. (25–26)

We need to bear in mind that the 'either' and the 'or' of structuralism's binary logic are not mutually exclusive. Rather, the one element of each of these oppositions necessarily includes the opposing element. As Jameson (1972) states "in language the perception of identity is the same as the perception of difference; thus every linguistic perception holds in its mind at the same time an awareness of its own opposite" (35). The two terms of a binary opposition logically imply and presuppose one another on every occasion. Crucially, for the structuralists, binary logic cannot be escaped.

So expectation was revived, to lend anxiety to my days. The Galaxy turned like an omelet in its heated pan, itself both frying pan and golden egg; and I was frying, with it, in my impatience.

But, with the passing of the galactic years, space was no longer that uniformly barren and colorless expanse. The idea of fixing with signs the points where we passed—as it had come to me and to Kgwgk—had occurred to many, scattered over billions of planets of other solar systems, and I was constantly running into one of these things, or a pair, or even a dozen simple two-dimensional scrawls, or else three-dimensional solids (polyhedrons, for example), or even things constructed with more care, with the fourth dimension and everything. So it happened that I reached the point of my sign, and I found five, all there. And I wasn't able to recognize my own. It's this one, no, that; no, no, that one seems too modern, but it could also be the most ancient; I don't recognize my hand in that one, I would never have wanted to make it like that . . . And meanwhile the Galaxy ran through space and left behind those signs old and new and I still hadn't found mine.

With this moment, Q's subject position as the one who creates signs, and thus, pure meaning, is no longer merely in question: it can never again be asserted. The frequency of the creation of signs insures that Q alone will not have the power to instill meaning. It also suggests that Q need not have been the maker of the "first" sign. As for that "first" sign—it doesn't exist. Where Q thought to find 'his' sign he found signs, none of them with Q's own identifiable stamp. The sign is no longer synonymous with name, power, dominion. It is one sign in a world of signs.

Importantly, however, it is also Q's contribution to language. The signs' differences allow for communication. Q may have lost the illusion of being the prime maker of meaning; nonetheless, he is able, if only for a hypothetical synchronic moment in space, to be where there are a definable five signs. Q is thus able to look at the structure of a language consisting of those five signs for that moment, and to 'read' those signs. Such a reading is determined by the differences between those signs, so Q reads in terms of modern/ancient and mine/not mine, for example. But, although it is closed, the synchronic state is temporary, and the movement of diachronic time (the galaxy running through space) necessitates ever-changing synchronic states. Even this temporary luxury of a methodological halt to affix meaning will soon be lost to Q, however, as the following passage moves us into a postmodern world.

I'm not exaggerating when I say that the galactic years that followed were the worst I had ever lived through. I went on looking, and signs kept growing thicker in space; from all the worlds anybody who had an opportunity invariably left his mark in space somehow; and our world, too, every time I turned, I found more crowded, so that world and space seemed the mirror of each other, both minutely adorned with hieroglyphics and ideograms, each of which might be a sign and might not be: a calcareous concretion on basalt, a crest raised by the wind on the clotted sand of the desert, the arrangement of the eyes in a peacock's tail (gradually, living among signs had led us to see signs in countless things that, before, were there, marking nothing but their own presence; they had been transformed into the sign of themselves and had been added to the series of signs made on purpose by those who meant to make a sign), the fire-streaks against a wall of schistose rock, the four-hundred-and-twenty-seventh groove—slightly crooked—of the cornice of a tomb's pediment, a sequence of streaks on a video during a thunderstorm (the series of signs was multiplied in the series of the signs of signs, of signs repeated countless times always

*the same and always somehow different because to the purposely
made sign you had to add the sign that had happened there by
chance), the badly inked tail of the letter R in an evening newspaper
joined to a thready imperfection in the paper, one among the eight
hundred thousand flakings of a tarred wall in the Melbourne docks,
the curve of a graph, a skid-mark on the asphalt, a chromosome
. . . Every now and then I'd start: that's the one! And for a second
I was sure I had rediscovered my sign, on the Earth or in space, it
made no difference, because through the signs a continuity had
been established with no precise boundaries any more.*

*In the universe now there was no longer a container and a
thing contained, but only a general thickness of signs superimposed
and coagulated, occupying the whole volume of space; it was constantly being dotted, minutely, a network of lines and scratches
and reliefs and engravings; the universe was scrawled over on all
sides, along all its dimensions. There was no longer any way to
establish a point of reference: the Galaxy went on turning but I
could no longer count the revolutions, any point could be the point
of departure, any sign heaped up with the others could be mine,
but discovering it would have served no purpose, because it was
clear that, independent of signs, space didn't exist and perhaps had
never existed.*

With the explosion of signs, of information, and of signifiers the
postmodern world asserts its particular order of things. Even the
definition of sign as signified/signifer no longer completely holds, as
each signified pointed to by a signifier is just as easily viewed as a
signifier itself, pointing elsewhere as well. Briefly, this is the move
from structuralism to poststructuralism, the latter of which is simultaneously an employment and a critique of structuralist thought.
Structuralism is based on closed systems of thought within which
meaning is determined by difference. Within these systems, as within
empiricist thought, then, the more information one has, the more
one is able to 'know'.[2] But when each signified becomes, in turn, a
signifier, when the system refuses to be closed, then having more
information does not necessarily assure one of fewer and clearer
answers. In a world of multiplying signs, as information increases,

definition decreases. Information leads to more information in a situation where "through the signs a continuity had been established with no precise boundaries." Boundaries are absolutely necessary for the difference thought of within structuralism's binary logic. Paradoxically, the lack of boundaries in Q's world provides us with the provisional framework of a poststructuralist view of meaning: the movement from difference to *différance* (see Chapter 2).

Actually, Q's final words send us in both structuralist and poststructuralist directions, which is not a contradiction, as the poststructuralists employ structuralist dictums within their critique. As a matter of fact, the highlighting of contradiction is in part the goal of one poststructuralist endeavor, deconstruction, most specifically described by Derrida's grammatology:

> the word "de-construction" is closely related . . . to the word "analysis," which etymologically means "to undo"—a virtual synonym for "to de-construct." The deconstruction of a text does not proceed by random doubt or generalized skepticism, but by the careful teasing out of warring forces of signification *within the text itself*. If anything is destroyed in a deconstructive reading, it is not meaning but the claim to unequivocal domination of one mode of signifying over another. (Johnson, 1981, xiv)

Poststructuralists within a postmodern world suspend the search for a scientific, unified meaning (even within the methodological fiction of synchrony). That does not mean that they are not concerned with the production of meaning; rather, the emphasis turns to that of power, chance, and paradigm: who determines meaning, how, and what form does it take, and for what purpose. Saussure's contributions to our vocabulary about language are useful as we think about our postmodern age precisely in terms of language and its arbitrariness. For one of the major postmodern questions has to do with the relationship between language and reality in our world. Q poignantly introduces the postmodern question with his last line: "Because it was clear that, independent of signs, space didn't exist and perhaps had never existed."

2

Critique of Representation
and J.M. Coetzee's *Foe*

When Saussure separated the referent from the sign, and posited an arbitrary and differential relationship between the sign's constituent parts (that is, between the concept—the signified, and the graphical or acoustical image of that concept—the signifier), he, in effect, provided a critique of representation. Representation is based on an essentially realistic epistemology; it "projects a mirror theory of knowledge and art, whose fundamental evaluative categories are those of adequacy, accuracy, and Truth itself" (Jameson, 1984a, viii). According to this epistemology there is a real world directly apprehensible by our consciousness, and through our language we are able to represent the truth of that world. Poststructuralist theory within the postmodern moment rejects the notion that 'reality' is directly apprehensible or that 'truth' is value-free. In the framework of the postmodern moment, neither the observer (the subject) nor the observed (the object) are autonomous entities; rather, they are culturally constituted, culturally interpreted, and mutually referential. Poststructuralism uses (and in the process, critiques) structuralism as it continues the critique of representation.

In order to understand better this critique, we may read J.M. Coetzee's novel, *Foe*, in conjunction with Jacques Derrida's essays,

"Structure, Sign and Play in the Discourse of the Human Sciences" and "Différance" as a means of reviewing the poststructuralist deconstruction of representation. I should note at the outset that the reading I extract from *Foe* ignores, for the time being, the obvious: Daniel Defoe's *Robinson Crusoe*. Although much of the power of Coetzee's work comes from a highlighting of the blindness (or in this case, the muteness) of Defoe's narrative, I pursue this relationship in Chapter 4, on intertextuality.

Much of *Foe* comes from the point of view of Susan Barton, the female castaway on Cruso's island. Part I of *Foe* is her written account, in the form of a letter to the author Foe whom she has met in England after her rescue from the island. She tells of how she came to be washed ashore; (briefly) of her history before her marooning—a daughter abducted in England, a search for the daughter in Brazil, an aborted return, alone, to Europe; and of the island, inhabited by Cruso and his tongueless slave Friday, both of whom were washed ashore years before. Barton's intention is to supply the author Foe with facts about the island so that he can turn the experience into a book. She describes the island's barrenness, Cruso's diligence in building terraces in the hopes that someday someone would come with seed to plant the terraces, her solitary walks, Friday's ritual of paddling a log to the site of his and Cruso's sunken ship in order to cast out flower petals, their rescue by an English ship a year after Barton is marooned, Cruso's death on board, and their coming, finally, to England.

Part II takes the form of letters from Barton to Foe. Her letters begin as perfunctory affairs, thanking Foe for money and answering his questions, but they soon become imaginings of Foe's surroundings and life as he writes. Not long thereafter she loses contact with Foe who has left his house to escape arrest as a debtor. Barton and Friday move into Foe's now-empty house, and she begins to write her own story: "The Female Castaway. Being a True Account of a Year Spent on a Desert Island. With Many Strange Circumstances Never Hitherto Related." Barton never stops writing to Foe, keeping the unsent letters stored in a chest near Foe's desk. She writes to Foe about her attempts to communicate with Friday, about how she believes Foe to be responsible for sending to her a girl who claims to be her daughter, and about how similar her life with Friday is to what it was on the island.

Part III, no longer in the epistolary mode, is Susan Barton's first-person account, in the present tense, relating what happens when she finds where Foe is hiding and goes to see him.

The last section, Part IV, begins with the same words as Part III as Susan Barton enters Foe's new dwelling: "the staircase was dark and mean." The narrator of this section is no longer Barton; rather, this "I" is outside of the story told thus far. The narrator finds Foe and Barton side by side in bed, and they are pictured as dead. The narrator discovers that Friday, lying in the corner, has a faint pulse, and presses his/her ear to the mute Friday's mouth: "from his mouth, without a breath, issue the sounds of the island." Then there is a break in the text and Part IV begins again. Again the narrator comes to the house, sees a plaque with the words *Daniel Defoe, Author*, enters the house and sees the couple in bed, face to face, and Friday on the floor. This time the narrator notes a chain scar around Friday's neck. The narrator opens the dispatch box next to Foe's desk and finds the first sheet of Barton's description to Foe of her story, which begins the novel with the words: "At last I could row no further." No longer reading, but continuing Barton's words, the narrator "with a sigh, making barely a splash, . . . slip[s] overboard" into the story, and finds himself/herself diving into the wreck of what had probably been a slave ship. The narrator's time is now 300 years after the sinking of the ship. In a corner of the captain's room is Friday. The narrator asks: "what is this ship?":

> But this is not a place of words. Each syllable, as it comes out, is caught and filled with water and diffused. This is a place where bodies are their own signs. It is the home of Friday. (Coetzee, 157)

What I haven't captured in this summary is the extent to which this novel is devoted to discussions about writing: what it means to write, who writes whose story, how, and what is the relationship between the stories told and 'reality' or 'truth'. Reverberating throughout these discussions is the question of the role of Friday's enforced silence. Susan Barton's expectations of what may be accomplished by writing, that is by presenting a story, are problematized as the novel progresses. She begins with the traditional point of view about telling "Cruso's story": she will recount what really happened, re-present 'truth'. Foe is then to add 'art' to her story. Art, to Barton, is "a liveliness" (Coetzee, 40) which will make the tale charming and interesting, but which need not affect the 'true' story of Cruso.

But Barton's difficulty with re-presenting the 'true' story begins immediately, as she writes:

> I would gladly now recount to you the history of this singular Cruso as I heard it from his own lips. But the stories he told me were so various, and so hard to reconcile one with another, that I was more and more driven to conclude age and isolation had taken their toll on his memory, and he no longer knew for sure what was truth, what fancy. (Coetzee, 11–12)

We see from the start then, that Cruso's story is to be told by Foe, by way of Barton, by way of her memory of stories told her by the now-absent Cruso who may not have known "what was truth, what fancy." This distancing of information from the 'source' disconcerts Barton, but does not keep her from believing that she can tell the 'true' story. She displays her faith in the written word when she tells the captain of the *John Hobart*, the ship that rescues her from the island: "I will not have any lies told." The captain, however, has less faith, if not in the word, at least in authors, responding: "There I cannot vouch for them . . . their trade is in books, not in truth" (Coetzee, 40).

After Barton completes her version of "Cruso's" story, which she sends to Foe, she begins a dialogue with herself (also in letters to Foe) on the role of authority: "Who but Cruso, who is no more, could truly tell you Cruso's story? I should have said less about him, more about myself" (Coetzee, 51). With this concern Barton introduces a crucial aspect of the critique of representation. The question isn't simply: can a 'reality' be re-presented exactly through language? But also: in the attempt at re-presentation, whose story gets told? To think of 'someone's story' is to think of 1) the events comprising the story to be told, and 2) the ownership or authority of the teller. This distinction becomes clearest later in the novel when Foe asks Barton to tell him more of her life in Bahia as she searched for her daughter. Barton's indignant reply is: "Bahia is not part of my story" (Coetzee, 115). In terms of the story which she is determined to tell, Bahia is not relevant. But in the more encompassing story which Foe seems determined to tell, Bahia is most certainly part of her story. The 'true' story in this case is defined not so much by what it contains, but by the teller, by the frame of reference. We remember structuralism's lesson on how meaning is defined *within* the boundaries of a system.

If it is the teller who determines what story gets told, then the teller must write from a position of some authority. But Barton, reflecting on her role, does not feel powerful:

> When I reflect on my story I seem to exist only as the one who came, the one who witnessed, the one who longed to be gone: a being without substance, a ghost beside the true body of Cruso. Is that the fate of all storytellers? (Coetzee, 51)

Barton posits the traditional opposition of substantial reality (the referent—here the true body of Cruso) and the ghostly representations (the sign) of the writer. The writer and her words are, in this equation, a mirror, reflecting a solid truth. The corpus of the author represents the substantial body of reality. There is, in this view, a knowable real world that may be directly mediated through the mirror of words. This is mimesis, the belief that there is an objective, real world that can be re-presented through words. And in this mimetic frame of reference, the fate of the storyteller is to be secondary, ghostly. On the other hand, Barton acknowledges the authority of Foe, to whom she pleads: "Return to me the substance I have lost, Mr Foe: that is my entreaty. For though my story gives the truth, it does not give the substance of the truth" (Coetzee, 51). Barton's plea shimmers between a traditional realist point of view about language and a poststructuralist view. On the one hand, her faith in the term 'truth' suggests something that is manifestly and unconditionally present and reachable through language. Her plea also suggests, however, that without the authority of another teller, her own subjectivity cannot be apprehended: she needs Foe to re-present her "substance." The suggestion here, that reality isn't mirrored by the words of the storyteller, but is, rather, brought to be by the teller, brings together two moments of critique within the postmodern moment: that our perception of reality takes place first within language, and second, within the particular social, cultural, historical positions of the teller.

This moment of rupture in Barton's faith is temporary, however, as we next hear Barton speaking to Friday (or rather, talking at him) about the power and magic of words in representing reality:

> Mr Foe has not met you, but he knows of you, from what I have told him, using words. That is part of the magic of words. Through the medium of words I have given Mr Foe the particulars of you and Mr Cruso and of my year on the island and the years you and Mr Cruso spent there alone, as far as I can supply them; ... Is writing not a fine thing, Friday? Are you not filled with joy to know that you will live forever, after a manner? (Coetzee, 58)

This is the empirical view of language as that which reproduces reality, added to the romantic view of language as the vehicle for immortality. We will leave, for the time being, the heavy irony of the notion of living forever in stasis for a slave whose tongue has been cut out by slavers, who spent his youth alone with a 'master' on an island, and is now living in a cellar in a foreign land, still, for all practical purposes, enslaved.

Barton's confidence in words again appears to mix a mimetic or representational view of language with the poststructuralist concept of people as constituted *by* language as much as they are constituting *of* language (Foucault, 1970), when she suggests that words would allow Friday to

> cross to the time before Cruso, the time before he lost his tongue, when he lived immersed in the prattle of words as unthinking as a fish in water; from where he may by steps return, as far as he is able, to the world of words in which you, Mr Foe, and I, and other people live. (Coetzee, 60)

This is, at first, a representational view of language as that medium which provides a passageway to reality. But the concept of living in a world of words, in which it is the words themselves that constitute reality, in which what Friday would get back to in getting back to a previous life would be words, that is the poststructuralist view. In other words, Barton's assumption about mimesis here includes its own critique. Some theorists suggest that the critique of the representation of language rests on "whether one considers the locus of meaning to be the world or to be language itself; or, in other terms, whether the world articulates language, or language articulates world" (Thiher, 1984, 92). Such a distinction may clarify what is at stake but it doesn't allow for the blurring of boundaries between world and language where much meaning takes place. That is to say: such an 'either/or' construct doesn't allow for the postmodern possibility that meaning may not lie in exactly one or the other frame of reference; rather, both world and language may be meaningful, and their meaning apprehensible, only in relation to one another. Later in this chapter I amplify, in Derridean theoretical terms, this idea of relationality, of meaning as 'between'.

From this point on Barton relies less on a belief in the possibility of direct apprehension of truth or reality, and instead, identifies an organizational principle to help her define what can and cannot be told. I refer here to her increasing emphasis on the importance of Friday's muteness:

> Then there is the matter of Friday's tongue. On the
> island I accepted that I should never learn how Friday
> lost his tongue, as I accepted that I should never learn
> how the apes crossed the sea. But what we can accept
> in life we cannot accept in history. To tell my story and
> be silent on Friday's tongue is no better than offering a
> book for sale with pages in it quietly left empty. Yet the
> only tongue that can tell Friday's secret is the tongue he
> has lost! (Coetzee, 67)

Once again we see Barton's acceptance, despite her problems thus
far, of the individual as somehow being able to re-present his/her
own life through language. What is new here is the role of Friday's
silence—presented as 'lack' of a tongue, and thus 'lack' of speech—
in the presentation of Barton's story. On one level, this is a reference
to the lost ability of a people, of Friday as slave, to speak. On a
linguistic level, however, Barton's reference here is to the role that
silence, lack, absence, otherness (what we will shortly be discussing
in the poststructuralist term, *différance*) plays in our apprehension
of meaning.

In her attempt to find out the 'truth' of how Friday lost his
tongue, Barton draws pictures which attempt possible representations
of the deed. Here, most concretely, she faces a realization about the
slippage or play within modes of representation:

> (Friday might not know the meaning of the word
> *truth*, I reasoned; nevertheless, if my picture stirred some
> recollection of the truth, surely a cloud would pass over
> his gaze; for are the eyes not rightly called the mirrors
> of the soul?)
> Yet even as I spoke I began to doubt myself. For if
> Friday's gaze indeed became troubled, might that not be
> because I came striding out of the house, demanding that
> he look at pictures, something I had never done before?
> Might the picture itself not confuse him? (Coetzee, 68)

Here is a recognition that no representation is pure or transparent, but that rather, the information received depends at the very least on the assumptions and projections of the representational method, as well as on the assumption that the method will have the same meaning from party to party:

> "Is this a faithful representation of the man who cut out your tongue?"—was that what Friday, in his way, understood me to be asking? If so, what answer could he give but No? And even if it was a Moor who cut out his tongue, his Moor was likely an inch taller than mine, or an inch shorter; wore black or blue, not white; was bearded, not clean-shaven; had a straight knife, not a curved one; and so forth. (Coetzee, 70)

Barton's attempts to communicate with Friday, like her attempts to tell "Cruso's story," consistently reveal some of the shortcomings and maneuverings of a representational paradigm. Her discomfort increases as she realizes the self-creative potential of language in another one-sided conversation with Friday:

> Oh, Friday, how can I make you understand the cravings felt by those of us who live in a world of speech to have our questions answered! It is like our desire, when we kiss someone, to feel the lips we kiss respond to us. . . .
>
> Be assured, Friday, by sitting at your bedside and talking of desire and kisses I do not mean to court you. This is no game in which each word has a second meaning, in which the words say "Statues are cold" and mean "Bodies are warm," or say "I crave an answer" and mean "I crave an embrace." (Coetzee, 79)

Barton appears to protest too much, as she struggles against a recognition of the protean multiplicity of language, in which words incorporate at least simultaneous and second meanings. She says that she means only to speak in similitudes, but we have learned from structuralism that the very concept of the similitude brings into the picture an 'other'. The meaning of "Statues are cold" includes, and takes place within the difference, the space, between that phrase and "Bodies are warm." In Barton's historical and cultural setting, however, she has no recourse but to blame her lack of authorial skill, not language itself:

> Alas, my stories seem always to have more applications than I intend, so that I must go back and laboriously extract the right application and apologize for the wrong ones and efface them. Some people are born storytellers; I, it would seem, am not. (Coetzee, 81)

Within the postmodern moment we disagree with Barton's conclusion. Each of us, within language, has no choice but to be a storyteller.

But that doesn't leave the speaker without power; Barton recognizes that power is part of language's equation when she speaks to Foe:

> You err most tellingly in failing to distinguish between my silences and the silences of a being such as Friday. Friday has no command of words and therefore no defence against being re-shaped day by day in conformity with the desires of others. I say he is a cannibal and he becomes a cannibal; I say he is a laundryman and he becomes a laundryman. What is the truth of Friday? You will respond: he is neither cannibal nor laundryman, these are mere names, they do not touch his essence, he is a substantial body, he is himself, Friday is Friday. But that is not so. . . . What he is to the world is what I make of him. Therefore the silence of Friday is a helpless silence. . . . Whereas the silence I keep regarding Bahia and other matters is chosen and purposeful: it is my own silence. (Coetzee, 121–22)

Barton has come a long way from her earlier reliance on truth as simply that which is represented by way of the mirror of words. Hers is now a discourse on power, a recognition of the ideological under-pinnings of representation: who is allowed to speak, for whom, and to what purpose? She puts her finger exactly on this question of control when she states: "It is still in my power to guide and amend. Above all, to withhold. By such means do I still endeavour to be father to my story" (Coetzee, 122). In referring to herself as "father," Barton emphasizes her position of authority. She continues to make the relationship between power and language clear when she says that the moral of a story Foe tells her "is that he has the last word who disposes over the greatest force" (Coetzee, 124). And thus, in bringing together the terms of force, power, father, and story, she identifies the link between the rationales of representation and logocentrism: the power of God, as the Father, embodies full Presence. This Presence is perceived as without lack, as an absolute and full Truth, as the Word, the Law.

Barton recognizes, finally, that to take control of a particular discourse is as close as one gets to controlling the depiction of one's life. Yet her final speeches indicate the precariousness of the power of telling one's own story (and we note that there is no longer the suggestion that "to tell one's own story" is synonymous with a simple truth). Barton says to Foe:

> I am not a story, Mr Foe. I may impress you as a story because I began my account of myself without preamble, . . . I choose not to tell [the life's story Foe wishes to hear] because to no one, not even to you, do I owe proof that I am a substantial being with a sub-stantial history in the world. . . . I am a free woman who asserts her freedom by telling her story according to her own desire. (Coetzee, 131)

Although, once again, Barton's assertions remind us of the one in this novel who cannot assert his freedom by telling his own story, for the time being we stay with Barton, who, shortly after the pre-ceding speech, begins to no longer trust in her own authorship:

> In the beginning I thought I would tell you the story
> of the island and, being done with that, return to my
> former life. But now all my life grows to be story and
> there is nothing of my own left to me. . . . Nothing is
> left to me but doubt. I am doubt itself. Who is speaking
> me? Am I a phantom too? To what order do I belong?
> And you: who are you? (Coetzee, 133)

These are, finally, poststructuralist questions about language and the
locus of power. No longer is Barton someone who speaks of the story
as that which represents truth or reality through language; rather,
she speaks of her own life as story, as spoken, as first constituted by
language, then shaped by a teller, and then reshaped by an audience,
as her final question to Foe makes clear.

As an 'author' within this novel, Foe is immediately suspect as
someone who tampers with 'reality', but where does his discourse
position itself within the world of *Foe*: does he believe that his words
can represent absolute 'truth', does he see himself as someone who
creates worlds through language, or does he recognize what we speak
of in the postmodern moment as the use-value of local and provisional 'truths'? Although most of what we know about Foe comes
from Barton's point of view, Foe as author is consistently presented
as godlike, and thus, as representing a traditional logocentric world
view. Barton provides the analogy between Foe and God early on
when she says, speaking of Foe's supposed menagerie of characters:
"In Mr Foe's house there are many mansions" (Coetzee, 77), re-
phrasing Christ's proclamation that "In my Father's house are many
mansions" (*John* 14:2). But this points the reader in a couple of
directions. In the first, more traditional, view, this reinforces the
concepts of Author as God the Father, as full Presence, and thus as
the purveyor of ultimate Truth, the Word, the Law. On the other
hand, if the author is godlike, then he or she need not be tied to an
empirical world, and may create, within the possibilities of language,
new worlds. In this latter, more postmodern view, the author recognizes that he/she cannot absolutely control the production and
reception (that is, the meaning) of language, the only tool at hand.

The creator is released from the controlling mimetic agenda and welcomes the opened space for play. We need to look closely at some of Foe's statements to see where he, as an author in the early 1700s, is situated.

Although much of Foe's discussion revolves around terms or concepts which resonate within a postmodern paradigm—blindness and silence—his world view is deeply dependent on a Christian logocentrism, while Barton, unknowingly, posits the poststructuralist-like questions. Foe's terminology is heavily loaded with Christian terms, as would be expected in early eighteenth-century England, when he says that in his own process of writing books he has often been lost in doubting, so that he is in the habit of planting a marker so that in his wanderings he has something to which he can return. He says that that marker is itself a sign of his blindness and incapacity, but at least he is heartened to be able to get back to it. He asks Barton:

> Have you considered . . . that in your own wander-
> ings you may, without knowing it, have left behind some
> such token for yourself; . . . which is the sign of blindness
> I have spoken of; and that, for lack of a better plan, your
> search for a way out of the maze . . . might start from
> that point and return to it as many times as are needed
> till you discover yourself to be saved? (Coetzee, 136)

This speech, however, also provides the tools with which to pry out of, at least temporarily, the Christian logocentric notion of Presence ("I was lost, but now am found"), and these tools are provided in the notion of blindness and silence. For we notice that this reference point which provides direction and thus meaning is not really a point (a presence) at all, but is rather, a moment of blindness and incapacity, a silence, an absence. Remember how in "A Sign in Space" Q thinks of his 'first' sign as a means of marking, not just time and place, but of meaning and presence as well. And when he comes to realize that this marker, instead, denotes a place of loss and absence (due to Kgwgk's erasure), that (erased) marker is nonetheless still the site of meaning. Once again, in *Foe*, we need to look at how silence or absence provides the space in which meaning is located. Does Foe mean to return Barton to Friday who is her point of reference as well as her point of blindness—a space of silence? With this in mind we hear a conflicting message in the following Foe speech: "In every story there is a silence, some sight concealed, some word unspoken, I believe. Till we have spoken the unspoken we have not come to the heart of the story" (Coetzee, 14). His first sentence suggests that there is within every story, within language, a silence, blindness, the unspoken. To make this point is to acknowledge that language, each word, and thus, each concept, carries within it all other words and concepts that are 'other', that are different from it. The concept of 'silence' is not just the opposite of 'sound'; it incorporates this opposing concept within it. Without the concept of 'sound', 'silence' is meaningless. Without the concept of 'sight', 'blindness' is meaningless. Within the word 'sight' is the word 'blindness'. Each word differs from *and* incorporates its opposite: the unspoken oppose as well as inhabit language. This is a poststructuralist recognition. But the sentence of Foe's which follows—that we need to speak the unspoken in order to come to the heart of the story—doesn't acknowledge that each time we speak we speak the unspoken. Foe here suggests the representational view that there is a presence that may be silent, a 'heart' that may be hidden, which words bring to light, represent in its centered fullness. According to this way of looking at language, each word does not reflect and acknowledge all other words, but rather, has a unitary wholeness, a pure, singular meaning. Foe completes the representational analogy with the organic metaphor of this unspoken essence as the 'heart'.

Both Foe and Barton come to think of Friday's island ritual of paddling a log onto the ocean to strew petals over the sunken ship as the moment of silence which needs to be spoken in order to give meaning to their stories. Foe then shifts the metaphor: "I said the heart of the story . . . but I should have said the eye, the eye of the story. . . . He rows across [the eye from the floor of the sea] and is safe. To us he leaves the task of descending into that eye" (Coetzee, 141). (When Foe talks about "the eye of the story" we hear the flutter of eye/I. See Chapter 3 for a critique of subjectivity, that is, a critique of the cultural construction and interpretation of the individual as subject that is often concurrent with the critique of representation in poststructuralist thought.) This shift in metaphor reaffirms the validation of the visual inherent in a representational schema, that is, in a correspondence theory of truth in which the truth or falsity of a statement can be *seen* by comparing the statement with the world. Barton shifts the metaphor yet again:

> Or like a mouth. . . . It is for us to descend into the mouth (since we speak in figures). It is for us to open Friday's mouth and hear what it holds: silence, perhaps, or a roar, like the roar of a seashell held to the ear. (Coetzee, 141–42)

This is a problematic moment in the text of *Foe*. On the one hand this may be read as a moment of clarity and bravery for Barton, as she realizes that it is Friday's silence that has directed the meaning of all her story up to this point and that she must listen to that silence. Barton appears to acknowledge her own inability to control the story. She recognizes that her story doesn't represent a fullness to which she need only give words, but rather that its very constitution is silence. Such a linguistic recognition is shot through with ideological implications: this is a moment in which Barton appears to abdicate the power and force of representation. Nonetheless, we must note the power relationship suggested by Barton's words. To "descend" into Friday's mouth is to speak in the figure of penetration. There is an element of force in the suggestion that they "open Friday's mouth." Also, by filling in, and thus limiting, the possibilities of what she would hear, Barton remains the determining subject and Friday the object. Similarly, Foe's statement that "We must make Friday's silence speak, as well as the silence surrounding Friday," suggests a position of force, of power. Although Barton asks "who will dive into the wreck?" of Friday's silence, we see that it can be neither Foe nor Barton, for, as their stories end, they still believe that Friday must speak (write) in their words. Barton's story is, as she suspects, a prefiguring of another diver, of a narrator who dives into the wreck, but to listen, not to *make* someone speak.

Given the above, we are somewhat surprised to find within one of Foe's last speeches the most devastating pronouncement against belief in absolute representation, in which any thing (idea or material object) has a matching word which will make the thing present in speech:

> There is no need for us to know what freedom means, Susan. Freedom is a word like any word. It is a puff of air, seven letters on a slate. It is but the name we give to the desire you speak of, the desire to be free. What concerns us is the desire, not the name. . . . If we devote ourselves to finding holes exactly shaped to house such great words as *Freedom, Honor, Bliss,* I agree, we shall spend a lifetime slipping and sliding and searching, and all in vain. They are words without a home, wanderers like the planets, and that is an end of it. But you must ask yourself, Susan: as it was a slaver's strategem to rob Friday of his tongue, may it not be a slaver's strategem to hold him in subjection while we cavil over words in a dispute we know to be endless? (Coetzee, 149–50)

The recognition here is of how the attribution of absolute and representational power to words is always already pernicious. It is Barton who is blind to this much earlier in *Foe* when she says of Friday: "He does not know what freedom is. Freedom is a word, less than a word, a noise, one of the multitude of noises I make when I open my mouth" (100). Barton's mistake, of course, is to assume that just because the particular noise that issues from her mouth is meaningless to Friday, that he thus "does not know what freedom is." We know by now that there is no natural correspondence between things and the words that we use to label those things. More importantly, here, the lack of such freedom behind this desire is itself what defines the concept of freedom.[1]

I make the case in the following section for reading Friday's silence as functioning in *Foe* as a form of what Jacques Derrida has called *différance*. I've suggested above that Friday's silence infuses the speech of Barton, and functions as that which makes meaning possible in her stories: *différance* is that space, that location of otherness which allows meaning to take place. The notion of *différance* is quite specifically a critique of representation, a critique of the belief in the mimetic nature of language and life, of language as the mirror of the world. The one-to-one correspondence of names with things assumes a 'natural' relationship between them.[2] In a representational theory of language, caprice is one of language's sins; for Saussure, however, as we've seen, language's arbitrariness is its very essence. This may sound harmless enough, but the stakes in a critique of traditional representation are high. Such a critique calls into question the very basis of Western thought: it problematizes the notions of Truth and Reality, it shakes the foundation of 'knowledge', it acts as a destabilizing concept which increases the power of words (through their arbitrariness) at the expense of 'The Word'. Derrida points out that the history of Western metaphysics is a history of 'centers' which provide an understanding of (and make possible) the structures surrounding the concept of Truth, regardless of the form that Truth takes: for example, God, Law, the Word. Always, says Derrida, this center takes the form of Presence. Barbara Johnson (1981) explains this aspect of Derrida's thought:

> Western thought (metaphysics), says Derrida, has always been structured in terms of dichotomies or polarities: good vs. evil, being vs. nothingness, presence vs. absence, truth vs. error, identity vs. difference . . . speech vs. writing. . . . The second term in each pair is considered the negative, corrupt, undesirable version of the first, a fall away from it. Hence, absence is the lack of presence, evil is the fall from good, . . . [T]hese hierarchical oppositions privilege unity, identity, immediacy . . . presence. (viii)

I begin this discussion of Derrida's critique of representation with his article, "Structure, Sign and Play in the Discourse of the Human

Sciences" (1978).[3] It is perhaps useful to remember, as I follow Derrida's argument, that, as structuralism divided the sign from the referent, poststructuralism further distances the signifier from the signified. Derrida expands structuralism's critique of representation by introducing the idea of 'play' into the idea of structure. He points out that the separation between signified and signifier, although crucial, ultimately privileges the closure of structure. For Saussure, the relationship between signified and signifier may be arbitrary, but it is a stable affair within a synchronic moment. Saussure, thus, assumes a place where meaning rests, if only for a hypothetical moment. To Derrida, this does not acknowledge the 'play', the movement, the slippage between signifiers, that is, the movement by which each signifier's signified becomes itself a signifier.

Derrida begins by showing how structuralism's critique of representation itself fits in with the history of metaphysics by relying on the logocentric concept of the center:

> the structurality of structure . . . has always been neutralized or reduced, and this by a process of giving it a center or of referring it to a point of presence, a fixed origin. The function of this center was not only to orient, balance, and organize the structure—one cannot in fact conceive of an unorganized structure—but above all to make sure that the organizing principle of the structure would limit what we might call the *play* of the structure. (1978, 278)

The history of Western metaphysics may be thought of as a series of substitutions of center for center which receives different forms and names, all of which have designated an invariable presence, for example: essence, existence, substance, subject, transcendentality, consciousness, God, man, and so forth. Derrida indicates the moment and movement into poststructuralist thought when he suggests that although we have no choice but to remain within a logocentric system—because our language through which we apprehend the world, through which we think and speak, is itself logocentric—that, nonetheless, the project is available to us to attempt to think simultaneously outside (while within) that structure. Such a poststructuralist step is not easily taken when we consider the degree to which our thinking is controlled by language. As Derrida (1978) says:

> We have no language—no syntax and no lexicon—which is foreign to this history [of metaphysics]; we can pronounce not a single destructive proposition which has not already had to slip into the form, the logic, and the implicit postulations of precisely what it seeks to contest. (280–81)

Derrida suggests that one method of critique is to use all the old concepts of language within the domain of empirical discovery while denouncing their limits, treating them as tools "to destroy the old machinery to which they belong and of which they themselves are the pieces" (1978, 284). That is, although we cannot get outside of the metaphysics of language, we may still use language as a means of questioning its own basis of meaning. The idea is to preserve as an instrument something whose truth-value is criticized. To do so would be to refuse the idea of the naturalness of language, and to think instead in terms of usage, of function. To refuse the idea of naturalness is to begin thinking:

> that the center could not be thought in the form of a present-being, that the center had no natural site, that it was not a fixed locus but a function, a sort of nonlocus in which an infinite number of sign-substitutions came into play. This was the moment when language invaded the universal problematic, the moment when, in the absence of a center or origin, everything became discourse . . . that is to say, a system in which the central signified, the original or transcendental signified, is never absolutely present outside a system of differences. The absence of the transcendental signified extends the domain and play of signification infinitely. (Derrida, 1978, 280)

This is a rather full passage. When Derrida talks about the moment when "language invaded the universal problematic," when "everything became discourse" with the absence of a center or origin, he is speaking of the moment in which a belief in representation is no longer consistent with a recognition that words (language) do not naturally re-present things (that is, the original thing is not re-presented by its stand-in, the word); rather, words refer to other words. The result is an inflation of language. Reality is defined by the words chosen to describe it. This is what we mean when we say that reality exists as a function of the discourse that articulates it: we perceive what we know as reality through a particular system of references which in effect preconstitute the meaning of the world, and thus, the world itself. Although some of this we learned from structuralism, it is the developed concept of 'play' that most obviously moves beyond structuralist thought.

Derrida calls the field of language that of 'play', that is, a field of substitutions. Derrida suggests that instead of being an inexhaustible field, as is traditionally assumed, there is something missing from language. What is missing is "a center which arrests and grounds the play of substitutions." Without a center, the play of language (signifiers) becomes a dynamic of "*supplementarity*":

> One cannot determine the center and exhaust totalization because the sign which replaces the center, which supplements it, taking the center's place in its absence— this sign is added, occurs as a surplus, as a supplement. (Derrida, 1978, 287)

Instead of a representational matrix that posits a closed system of direct reference between thing and word, which is made possible by the presence of an organizing center (or Truth), we are now dealing with the sign which replaces the center (which is always already a sign). To say that the sign replaces the center is to note that the sign, that language, always represents a lack; it stands in for an absence. Language doesn't re-present the world; it is not a moment of simultaneity. Rather, language stands in for, presents, something that is not present. Language functions in the space of absence. That is why the "movement of supplementarity" is both in addition to *and* a substitute; it means to add to (to be superfluous) and to replace (to be necessary). When discourse enters the picture, that is, when the center—the transcendental signified—is never present, then language becomes movement. Language becomes a slippage from signifier to signifier, rather than from signifier to absolute signified. This is the "overabundance of the signifier" of which Derrida speaks. The signifier's "*supplementary* character, is thus the result of a finitude, that is to say, the result of a lack which must be supplemented" (1978, 290).

Derrida's use of the terms 'presence' and 'absence' can be confusing. When Derrida states that "Play is the disruption of presence," think of play as a concept of movement, of slippage. This is where Derrida is, for our purposes, clearest in distinguishing between traditional humanist representational thought and that of poststructuralist play:

> There are thus two interpretations of interpretation, of structure, of sign, of play. The one seeks to decipher, dreams of deciphering a truth or an origin which escapes play and the order of the sign, and which lives the necessity of interpretation as an exile. The other, which is no longer turned toward the origin, affirms play and tries to pass beyond man and humanism, the name of man being the name of that being who, throughout the history of metaphysics or of ontotheology—in other words, throughout his entire history—has dreamed of full presence, the reassuring foundation, the origin and the end of play. (1978, 292)

If we think of this 'play', this loss of the center, in a spirit of mourning for the lost dream of truth and absolutes, then we are not thinking within the postmodern moment. Within the postmodern moment 'play' remarks a "joyous affirmation": it suggests a world not based on a closing-down of meaning through a false acquiescence of power, but rather on an opening-up toward the privileging of active interpretation. The endless play of language and of meaning suggests a postmodern moment in which meaning is acknowledged to shift and to function for particular purposes. The emphasis may then be placed on the use-value of language and on the agency behind that use-value. As a result, the responsibility of interpretation is highlighted, as opposed to the humanist "dream" of reassuring foundation and presence.

It is the notion of what Derrida calls *différance* that suggests an alternative to thinking in terms of simple presence. In his essay, "Différance" (1982), Derrida's neologism *différance* is "literally neither a word nor a concept" (3), but functions, rather as a condition of possibility of meaning. He notes that the graphic difference—replacing an *e* with an *a* (*différance* instead of *difference*)—"is read, or it is written but it cannot be heard" (3). This is important in that the shift, the distinction, is silent: the

> silence of the graphic difference between the *e* and the *a* can function, of course, only within the system of phonetic writing, and within the language and grammar which is historically linked to phonetic writing as it is to the entire culture inseparable from phonetic writing. But I would say that this in itself—the silence that functions within only a so-called phonetic writing—quite opportunely conveys or reminds us that, contrary to a very widespread prejudice, there is no phonetic writing. (1982, 4–5)

Derrida's critique of Western metaphysics focuses on the metaphysical privileging of the spoken word over the written word. The image of perfectly self-present meaning of the spoken word (phonocentrism) is, according to Derrida, the underlying ideal of Western culture. This belief in the self-presentation of meaning is not only phonocentric, but logocentric. Writing—the physical markings on the page—on the other hand, is considered by the logocentric system to be merely a representation of speech. Derrida doesn't reverse this value system—

rather, he attempts to show that opposing the terms of speech and writing on the basis of presence vs. absence, or immediacy vs. representation is impossible, since speech is *always already* structured by differences and distance as much as is writing. That is, the area between, or the slippage between, signified and signifier is where meaning takes place in speech as well as in writing.

This discussion of phonocentrism also takes place within *Foe*. Remember Foe's suggestion to Barton that she teach Friday to write. Barton presents the phonocentric, logocentric viewpoint when she responds: "How can he write if he cannot speak? Letters are the mirror of words. Even when we seem to write in silence, our writing is the manifest of a speech spoken within ourselves or to ourselves" (Coetzee, 142). This is the logocentric concept of speech as a direct conduit to, or representation of, thought, in which speech is primary and writing is a fallen manifestation of speech. Foe disagrees, and speaks of writing as something that precedes speech:

> Writing is not doomed to be the shadow of speech. Be attentive to yourself as you write and you will mark there are times when the words form themselves on the paper *de novo*, as the Romans used to say, out of the deepest of inner silences. We are accustomed to believe that our world was created by God speaking the Word; but I ask, may it not rather be that he wrote it, wrote a Word so long we have yet to come to the end of it? May it not be that God continually writes the world, the world and all that is in it? (Coetzee, 142–43)

Ultimately, Foe's assumptions, too, are deeply logocentric, as they continue to derive the authority of writing from the Word of God; this is only to be expected from a British voice in the early 1700s. However, Foe's point of view also suggests a poststructuralist sense of open-endedness, of supplementarity, although for Foe this supplementarity is ultimately contained by God.

We need to keep this discussion of speech and writing in mind as we read Derrida's discussion of *différance* and silence:

> the play of difference, which, as Saussure reminded us,
> is the condition for the possibility and functioning of
> every sign, is in itself a silent play. Inaudible is the dif-
> ference between two phonemes which alone permits
> them to be and to operate as such. (1982, 5)

In order to recognize the importance of this inaudibility we need to
refer to a system that resists the opposition, crucial to Western metaphysics, between the sensible (that which may be directly appre-
hendible by the senses) and the intelligible (that which may be
'known'):

> The order which resists this opposition . . . is announced
> in a movement of *différance* between two differences or
> two letters, a *différance* which belongs neither to the
> voice nor to writing in the usual sense, and which is
> located . . . *between* speech and writing. (Derrida, 1982,
> 5)

Différance, for Derrida, is writing, but writing here does not refer
to the marks we make on the page. Rather, writing, as a necessary
precondition for speech refers to a space, to a moment of difference
which makes meaning possible. As a movement, or condition of possibility of meaning, *différance* is thus neither presence nor absence:
"[I]t has neither existence nor essence. It derives from no category
of being, whether present or absent" (1982, 6). It is that which makes
possible, in Jane Tompkins's (1988) words: "the presentation of
being-present, that is, the possibility of opposition" (741). *Différance*
is that which allows us to think in terms of contrast, to think relationally. Neither essence nor absence, it's what makes possible the
thought of the opposition of present/absent or being/non-being. *Différance*, explains Tompkins (1988),

> expresses the possibility of differentiation, the possibility
> of opposition, and so it doesn't belong to any realm that
> could be named as such. Why not? Because as soon as

you want to assign it to a realm, say of the sensible or the intelligible, or of any two pairs, you have abrogated what *différance* itself is, that which makes any such opposition come into being. *Différance* is something that cannot ever actually be given a name because as soon as you name it, you have unnamed it. (741)

Think of how Friday's silence functions in *Foe*. Barton tells Foe that "the story of Friday . . . is properly not a story but a puzzle or hole in the narrative (I picture it as a buttonhole, carefully cross-stitched around, but empty, waiting for a button)" (Coetzee, 121). Friday's muteness functions neither as absence (it is defined as "a puzzle or hole") nor as presence (it is "empty" and "waiting"), yet it is that which makes Barton think in terms of a button for the hole. This silence is a space, a moment which provides the need and the opportunity for Barton to speak and write within the space between hole and button.

Derrida clarifies *différance* by showing that it has two vectors: to differ ("to be not identical, to be other, discernible") and to defer ("the action of putting off until later"). Within the paradigm of representation the sign is "put in the place of the thing itself. . . . The sign represents the present in its absence. . . . The sign, in this sense, is deferred presence" (1982, 9). According to the representational paradigm, although the sign defers presence, the sign may be thought about only on the *basis* of the presence that it defers as it *moves toward* the deferred presence that it aims to reappropriate. Thus, says Derrida,

> the substitution of the sign for the thing itself is both *secondary* and *provisional*: secondary due to an original and lost presence from which the sign thus derives; provisional as concerns this final and missing presence toward which the sign in this sense is a movement of mediation. (1982, 9)

Derrida's project is to look at the consequences of opposing an 'originary' *différance* to the secondary and provisional characteristics of the sign. One consequence, says Derrida, is that, "One could no longer include *différance* in the concept of the sign, which always has meant the representation of a presence." And thus, the second consequence: "one puts into question the authority of presence, or of its simple symmetrical opposite, absence or lack" (1982, 9–10).

To gain a clearer sense of how *différance* functions, we need to remember, again, the principle of difference as the condition for signification at the foundation of structuralism (c-a-t signifies the furry animal to us because it is distinguished from c-a-p or b-a-t). But we move beyond simple differences to *différance* when we look at every concept as

> inscribed in a chain or in a system within which it refers to the other, to other concepts by means of the systematic play of differences. Such a play, *différance*, is thus no longer simply a concept, but rather the possibility of a conceptuality, of a conceptual process and system in general. . . . *Différance* is the non-full, non-simple, structured and differentiating origin of differences. Thus, the name "origin" no longer suits it. (Derrida, 1982, 11)

Our temptation throughout this discussion is to not be satisfied with perceiving *différance* as a space, as a condition of possibility for meaning, but to want to be able to say " '*différance*' is this" or " '*differance*' is that." Derrida anticipates this need when he says that "Differences, thus, are 'produced'—deferred—by *différance*. But what defers or who defers? In other words, what is *différance*?" (1982, 14). He points out, however, that to accept the form of this question ("what is?" "who is?") is to conclude that *différance* has been derived, has happened,

> is to be mastered and governed on the basis of the point of a present being, which itself could be some thing, a form, a state, a power in the world to which all kinds of names might be given, a *what*, or a present being as a *subject*, a *who*. (1982, 15)

But we have already learned that *différance* is not *being*, that to say what it *is* is to make it disappear. *Différance* is that which marks and makes possible the passage from one term of opposition to another, and which indicates that each term resides within the other. Derrida states that

> one could reconsider all the pairs of opposites on which philosophy is constructed and on which our discourse lives, not in order to see opposition erase itself but to see what indicates that each of the terms must appear as the *différance* of the other, as the other different and deferred in the economy of the same (the intelligible as differing-deferring the sensible, as the sensible different and deferred; . . . culture as nature different and deferred, differing-deferring). (1982, 17)

I refer again to Barton's one-sided discussion with Friday about her lack of control over language when she says to him that her words "Statues are cold" don't mean "Bodies are warm." Derrida's point is that the phrase "Statues are cold" *is* the phrase "Bodies are warm" different and deferred. These are not exclusionary opposites; one phrase is a constitutive alterity of the other. Meaning is located, given to, made available, to her phrase "Statues are cold" in this passage by the space, the *différance* between that phrase, and "Bodies are warm." Meaning, thus, takes place in movement, the movement by which signs defer to signs, a movement in which traces of other differing signs exist in every sign. Every meaning holds within itself the trace of those meanings from which it differs. Derrida's view of meaning as *différance*, as the infinite play of differing and deferring, constitutes, then, a most radical attack on a classical view of representation: there is no locus for meaning, only movement, dynamics, play.

I've been suggesting throughout this chapter that Friday functions in *Foe* as neither presence nor absence, but rather, as the *différance*, the condition of possibility for Barton's stories. How can I say that he doesn't signify presence? Isn't he as much of a character as Barton and Foe? Of course. My point is, however, that it is the position of Friday which makes possible the conceptual process which leads to Barton's stories. Friday is not presence (in Barton's frame of reference) because he is speechless and because he is a slave. (In the text of *Foe* to be speechless is to be powerless—a slave.) He is not absence because he is that palpable something whose history she tries to name. Friday's own story is not told in *Foe*. Friday is, rather, the condition of possibility for the stories that Barton tries to tell. Note how Barton, in the following passage, doesn't refer to Friday's silence as lack or absence, but as the shadow of a lack: "If the story seems stupid, that is only because it so doggedly holds its silence. The shadow whose lack you feel is there: it is the loss of Friday's tongue" (Coetzee, 117). The shadow is both presence differing and deferred from absence and vice versa. It is within this silence that Barton speaks. Most of the story of *Foe* is not of authors re-presenting things through language, but rather of authors becoming aware that the very initiative of language is silence. For Barton, Friday's silence functions as the metaphorical *différance*: it is Friday's silence that provides the impetus for the different stories she attempts, and the sense of their ever-deferring meaning. It is his silence which leads to the picture stories through which she attempts to suggest how he lost his tongue. It is his silence which provides the sense of deferred meaning, in that each attempt to speak of him is not seen as an ultimate truth, but rather, of yet another in a series of 'discourses'.

The analysis I provide here necessitates questions about, for example, the political implications of reading Friday as a condition of possibility rather than as a subject. To suggest that Friday's silence is somehow a positive thing because it makes space for Barton's stories would be an irresponsible interpretation. If Friday *weren't* silent, Barton would simply have other stories to tell. And quite clearly, Friday's silence is not the *différance* which makes possible his *own* story. In the world of *Foe*, only Barton's, and not Friday's story may be told. Although Foe and Barton quibble over their words, their stories, they never approach a meaning Friday would provide. This may be Coetzee's point as he ends the novel with the narrator discovering, as he kneels next to the drowned Friday, that "this is not a place of words. . . . This is a place where bodies are their own signs" (Coetzee, 157). Words are available only to the Bartons and the Foes.

Coetzee's ending to Foe is ambiguous when looked at in terms of representation. On the one hand, the above quote reinstates the body as the center which structures meaning, the body as transcendental signified. On the other hand, the narrator also critiques the belief that the body may be re-presented in its fullness by language: "this is not a place of words. Each syllable, as it comes out, is caught and filled with water and diffused" (Coetzee, 157). The point is that there is a reality; there are lived lives—to critique the theory of representation is not to suggest that we do not exist, and thus, that our lives aren't important—but these lives are only interpreted through language. And language is always discourse, loaded with cultural significance. Perhaps Foe suggests, through these conflicting possibilities, that there are situations when to speak for something or someone else, to interpret, to add the baggage of our own language to another body, is an act of irresponsibility. We aren't asked to 'interpret' Friday's body, but to listen to it. We are reminded, thus, of how the theory of representation is ideologically suspect: in its reliance on and belief in a central Truth and Reality, we need to ask whose truth is presented, and whose is excluded. Truth, history tells us, is determined by power. Any story Barton and Foe tell about Friday, despite their intentions, is suspect, because their definitions of truth are socially, culturally, historically loaded and determined. The 'truth' of a white woman and man in England in the eighteenth century cannot be synonymous with the 'truth' of the experience of a black, mutilated slave.

Perhaps this is one reason why the structure of Foe becomes so explicitly metafictional at the end, where someone from outside the work steps into the novel. Is the intruding narrator impatient with the stories of Foe and Barton? Impatient with their quibbling over words? Impatient with Friday's silence? If so, the metafictional strategies employed in Foe are yet another level of the critique of representation. Metafiction refers to fiction which calls attention to itself

as an artifact in order to raise questions about the relationship between fiction and reality (Waugh, 1984). In a novel in the realistic
tradition of mimesis, we would not have an intrusion by someone
outside the text's frame of reference into the very fabric of the novel,
nor would we have the form of eternal regress we get in the structure
of the novel, in which a segment doesn't come to closure but instead
is repeated, with a variation, with a spiraling outward, out of the
novel. The various receding and interwoven levels of narrative presented by *Foe* suggest Derrida's discussion of an endless chain of
signifiers, in which there is no final 'truth' or transcendental signified:
each signified becomes a pointing signifier. For example, the 'novel'
Foe is to write (as signifier) points to the written account Barton
gives him (as signified). But Barton's account is also the signifier of
Cruso's story, which is then the signified. But Cruso's story, we remember, will not solidify as transcendental signified because his varying memories blur the boundary between "truth" and "fancy." Add
to this some of the other narratives pointed to by this novel—*Robinson Crusoe* or the accounts of Andrew Selkirk (the castaway on
whom Defoe is supposed to have 'based' *Robinson Crusoe*)—and we
see that signified and signifier are hardly a stable affair.

   Foe is both an insistence on the substance of Friday, as well as
a recognition that we can only contextualize Friday's story within
the "prison-house" of language (Jameson, 1972). A project such as
Coetzee's brings to mind Alan Thiher's (1984) comment to the effect
that although most postmodern writers have given up on finding
revelation, salvation, or transcendence in fiction, they have not necessarily given up on claims for literature as a form of knowledge.
Although we do not have direct access to someone's reality—because
social, historical, cultural, and linguistic texts intervene, so that all
stories are 'about', finally, the language through which the stories
are presented—that doesn't mean that there isn't a reality, a lived life,
that takes place.

   The final lines of *Foe* leave the text in a postmodern openness,
as the 'reality' of Friday washes over the narrator through silence,
not language. Thus, the narrator is not called upon to provide closure,

that is, to interpret Friday's silence into a final meaning, but rather, to listen:

> His mouth opens. From inside him comes a slow stream, without breath, without interruption. It flows up through his body and out upon me; it passes through the cabin, through the wreck; washing the cliffs and shores of the island, it runs northward and southward to the ends of the earth. Soft and cold, dark and unending, it beats against my eyelids, against the skin of my face. (Coetzee, 157)

Barton and Foe have been unable to "make" Friday speak, or to hear his silence because that silence could not be heard within their particular cultural paradigms. The narrator from another time has to give up control in order to hear Friday, and what s/he hears is not language as we know it; nevertheless, the "slow stream" contains a powerful text. The stream that flows up through Friday's body does not come in the form of words meant to re-present his experience. The narrator and the reader are no longer in the position of power in which they provide interpretations based on their own ideological, cultural, historical contexts and desires. To 'hear' Friday's silence is to resist the closure of ultimate interpretation for the sake of possible 'other' stories.

3

Critique of Subjectivity and Michel Tournier's *Friday*

PART I: *The Subject as Construct*

In J.M. Coetzee's *Foe* Susan Barton and Foe speak of the silence of Friday's story that must be spoken before they can come to the heart of that story. But then Foe says: "I said the heart of the story . . . but I should have said the eye, the eye of the story. . . . To us he leaves the task of descending into that eye" (Coetzee, 141). And that is, quite specifically, the task before Barton and Foe: to descend into the 'I' of Friday to identify what has constituted Friday as a subject within their particular cultural and historical situation—that is, to identify Friday's subject position in the world of Barton and Foe, and to also identify their role in the construction and maintenance of that subject position.

When we use the word 'subject' we introduce a series of concepts that, while possibly coterminous, are not necessarily synonymous. On occasion 'the subject' is used to mean 'the individual'. The term 'individual' carries with it a sense of one who is unified, whole, the source of conscious action; it is this 'individual' who is the subject of much psychological discourse. The 'subject' for a certain kind of psychoanalysis, however, refers to "the complex of psychical formations which are constituted as the human being is positioned in relation to language" (Smith, 1988, xxxiii). To be a 'subject' is also to be 'subject to' and as such is positioned in terms of ideology as well as language. Related to the concept of 'subject-to' or 'subjected' is the 'subject position', which refers to ways one is ascribed a 'position' within various discourses. For example, we are each assigned a subject position according to gender, race, ethnicity, family, region, as well as according to a variety of other discourses (as a woman, as white, as Irish, as daughter, as a Midwesterner, as a consumer, etc.). Each of these subject positions is a part of the 'individual' who inhabits them: "yet they never cohere to form a complete and non-contradictory 'individual'—let alone an 'individual' who determines the character or constitution of his/her own subjectivity" (Smith, 1988, xxxiv).

Thus, to critique subjectivity is not to refuse the concept of the subject in any of its definitions; that would be an exercise in futility. The poststructuralist critique of subjectivity is wide-ranging and multifarious, but is most consistently an impulse to look at the historical, philosophical, and cultural construction of the subject. It is to look at the human being as neither totally subjected or constituted (that is, determined completely by the social or linguistic structures around him/her), nor totally individualistic or constituting (that is, the source or agent of all meaning), but rather, as both constituted *and* constituting.[1] A critique of subjectivity may take as its starting point psychoanalysis, feminist theory, Marxist theory, or semiotics, for example. But the bottom line is an insistence that our readily accepted, commonsensical, and supposedly timeless humanist view of the normal 'man'—as the rational individual—is the result of a particular set of cultural constructions.

To understand the critique of subjectivity underway within our postmodern moment we return once again to a basic structuralist principle, which has its roots in Marxism: how something is perceived (in this case the subject—who it is) is determined by the social and cultural patterns which shape it. As such, structuralism critiques the humanist notion of the individual as causal, as the origin and the destination of history. This is a crucial beginning to poststructuralism's debate on the subject. Derrida, for example, moves from this point to his discussion of the center in "Structure, Sign and Play in the Discourse of the Human Sciences," which is a critique of subjectivity as well as of representation. Furthermore, each poststructuralist hearkens back to Saussure's crucial proposition that the subject in its consciousness of itself as a subject is inscribed in language. The subject becomes a 'speaking' subject only by making its speech conform to the system of rules of a language.

For many theorists, regardless of their professional orientation or political agenda, structuralism's tenets become too deterministic, too much given to closure. More and more frequently the question of historical change is introduced, as theorists attempt to think of the subject as being an agent of history, without reintroducing the humanist individual. For example, the question arises: if all experience is mediated by language (which in itself may be social in nature), if the individual is not a pregiven entity, but an 'always-already social' being, then who or what is responsible for the structures in place, and how do these structures change? For many theorists the project is specifically to account for change without introducing the subject; for others, the issue of agency and responsibility is paramount. Before giving some examples of how this 'who' or 'what' is discussed today from a variety of positions or agendas, I first provide a brief historical/chronological look at various perceptions of the subject. My point in this brief survey isn't to suggest an unbiased account of how the subject brings about change, but rather to suggest that as a result of change, the concept of the subject and his/her role shifts.[2] The purpose of such a survey is to emphasize the position of the subject as an historically specific construct. Although a variety of labels may be given to particular chronological periods, there is general agreement about some of the moments which have come to be identified with our modern subject. The danger of such a survey is that it may seem to indicate some type of logical progression through time toward the subject of today. Rather than a progression, however, many theorists see change in the form of 'ruptures' or 'events'.[3]

Although we are used to taking for granted as 'natural' the 'I' of the rational individualist who constitutes the humanist subject, the consciousness of the medieval subject, for example, was pretty much synonymous with his/her position in a hierarchy based on a feudal and theocentric world order: life on earth was a mere foreshadowing of the life to come, precluding any sense of interiorization, and thus, for the most part, individualization, in our 'modern' sense of the word. For another example, around the end of the fifteenth century, and with the Renaissance, the value of the here and now was heightened and with it the status of the individual. During the later Reformation, human life and the soul's salvation were seen as resting precisely on the autonomous behavior of the individual.

The accepted 'birth of the human subject' as a distinct presence with specific attributes is commonly dated as occurring in the seventeenth century and is associated with Descartes: the act of doubting everything and anything as an act of thought could at least assure the certainty of the subject's own being (*cogito ergo sum*/ I think therefore I am). Thus, Descartes set thinkers on the path of reifying this thinking subject who searched for certainty and Reason, which then becomes the source of knowledge and of truth.

Couze Venn (1984, 133–34) discusses various conditions of possibility for the notion of the *cogito*, that is, for the mind guaranteeing its own basic rationality. Venn gives one condition of possibility as the Copernican revolution (in the early sixteenth century) which decentered the Earth from the center of the cosmos and thus transformed the scientific, epistemological, ontological, and ideological principles of that era which functioned together to make sense of the world. He points to the work of Galileo as the symbolic turning point in the transformation of the basis of Western rationality because it summarizes the redefinition of scientific intelligibility that marks modern science; that is, it elaborates a conceptual system in which *rational* necessity takes the place of physical causality.

A second condition of possibility for the modern notion of the *cogito*, according to Venn, is the principle of order founded in mathematics, and an ideology emerging from the seventeenth century that views all science and all reason as masculine, powerful, productive, and belonging to *this* world. A third condition of possibility is the shift which locates Reason and the Subject-of-Reason as the ultimate guarantee of this principle of order. Thus, logic and rationality come to be regarded as the basic elements of the logocentric subject.

Although we can never speak of a time in the history of 'man' without speaking of a subject, not until Descartes do we begin to speak of that human subject which we take for granted today. For Descartes the mind is conceptualized in the same terms as other physical entities; the mind is subject to laws in the same way as the material world. The result of this view is the concept of the 'normal' subject. Ideally, the model is the male, European, propertied, Christian individual; women, children, and the propertyless, for example, were excluded from the model on the basis of the supposed inability of these groups (or subject positions) to make rational judgments. This simultaneous normalization and exclusion has led to critiques of this humanist subjectivity from, for example, feminists and Marxists, who have pointed out that this 'unexamined' norm reproduces social relations and relations of power as they are played out in social institutions of all kinds. In short, the 'normal' subject is a construction. This is often a difficult point to grasp, quite simply because this norm is considered simple common sense; what we may fail to understand is that what passes for common sense is also a cultural construct. We are caught in a tautology: we think something is 'normal' because it's normal to think of it that way.

Although this subject as the rational individual, first theorized in the seventeenth century, is still with us today, 'he' has undergone some changes and challenges. Ellie Ragland-Sullivan (1986) states that, for example, the advent of Romanticism brought with it a further elevation of the subject: "For the Romantics, the 'I' was the seat of emotion, creativity, intuition, imagination, mystical unity with the Absolute—the source of all that was Good and True—and so able to transcend reason and understanding" (9).[4] The Romantic 'I' was, in the words of Ragland-Sullivan, 'dethroned' by the challenge of Darwin's theory of evolution in the early 1900s. With Darwin, Nature becomes the origin and the foundation: all explanations have to find their basis in natural processes. These processes are described by science, so that the question of how we know that the natural processes are as we think them to be is answered by an appeal to scientific authority. At this point, then, the human subject is biologized and individualism becomes the norm because it is thought to accord to the *natural state* of existence (Venn, 1984, 144–45). However, this ideology also raised the status of external objects as determinants of human existence. In literary critical terms:

> Moving even beyond the controlling power of economic and social forces, Naturalists depicted the determination of genetic and biological forces and natural selection. The "I" had become the product of biomechanistic determination. (Ragland-Sullivan, 1986, 10)

Obviously, from the fourteenth to the nineteenth century, the 'I' was not a stable structure. Freud's contribution in the late nineteenth century was to posit the conscious mind as not in control of itself. The fact that unconscious mechanisms contribute to behavior—from slips of the tongue to psychoses—meant that the subject could no longer refer her/his 'identity' to rational consciousness and self-mastery. Dreams, the most irrational of events, became the 'key' to subjectivity. In short, Freud initiates the discourse of the decentering of the subject. Ultimately, says Ragland-Sullivan, despite an awareness that unseen forces affect behavior, "the twentieth-century Occidental subject is still a mixture of the medieval 'I' believe; the Cartesian 'I' think; the Romantic 'I' feel; as well as the existential 'I' choose; the Freudian 'I' dream, and so forth" (10).

The twentieth-century subject has more basically been associated with empirical science: the empirical subject believes in the objectivity of his/her own perceptions, and thus, seeks methods which prove, objectively, his/her hypotheses. Such a methodological linking of observation to the Cartesian privilege of reason has encouraged the empirical subject to deify science and technology. In short, we believe that through science and reason we have access to generalized truths. In turn, those truths become universal and provable, and thus normalizing. Instead of perceiving our assumptions as themselves determinate of what we accept as conclusions (that is, perceiving our paradigms as themselves responsible for and 'containing' their own conclusions), we twentieth-century Occidental humanist individuals believe that there is, on the one hand, the world or society which gives us facts and, on the other hand, the individual who uses science and reason to make sense of that world. As a result we find it virtually impossible to think outside the terms generated by the dualism of individual/society. The individual, as a concept, could not exist without its opposite number, society. This dualism underlies all humanist social sciences, from psychology to sociology to anthropology.

The humanist position tends to see the individual as the agent of all social phenomena and productions, including knowledge; it is the Cartesian subject in modern form. It is this unified, rational, controlled subject of humanism which leads to a questioning of the notion of the subject by contemporary theorists: by Jacques Lacan in psychoanalysis; by Roland Barthes in semiotics and cultural studies; by Louis Althusser in Marxist criticism; by Michel Foucault and Jacques Derrida in the history of knowledge and the production of discourse, to name but a few.[5]

For example, Louis Althusser in "Ideology and Ideological State Apparatuses" discusses subjectivity in terms of ideology. Althusser talks of ideology as a "material practice" in that it exists in the behavior of people acting according to their beliefs. Althusser provides the connection between ideology and our concern here, subjectivity:

> [W]here only a single subject (such and such an individual) is concerned, the existence of the ideas of his belief is material in that *his ideas are his material actions inserted into material practices governed by material rituals which are themselves defined by the material ideological apparatus from which derive the ideas of that subject....*
>
> I say: the category of the subject is constitutive of all ideology, but at the same time and immediately I add that *the category of the subject is only constitutive of all ideology insofar as all ideology has the function (which defines it) of "constituting" concrete individ-*

> *uals as subjects.* In the interaction of this double con-
> stitution exists the functioning of all ideology, ideology
> being nothing but its functioning in the material forms
> of existence of that functioning. (1971, 169, 171)

Ideology is thus the 'common sense' that we have been discussing,
existing in commonplaces as well as in philosophical and religious
systems. But, as Catherine Belsey in *Critical Practice* (1980) points
out, ideology is also "a set of omissions, gaps rather than lies, smooth-
ing over contradictions, appearing to provide answers to questions
which in reality it evades" (57). That is, ideology obscures its own
constructedness by means of its appeal to the commonsensical, the
natural, the self-evident.

Althusser also refers to the subject in a manner which will be
important in the next section of this chapter (on Foucault's "The
Subject and Power"): The subject, says Althusser, is a subjected being
who submits to the authority of the social formation as it represents
itself in ideology as the Absolute Subject; this Absolute Subject allows
for "the duplication of *the Subject into subjects*" (1971, 180). In
our culture this Absolute Subject is first recognized as God and is
then duplicated into positions such as the king, the boss, Man, conscience. For Althusser such duplication

> means that all ideology is *centred*, that the Absolute
> Subject occupies the unique place of the Centre, and
> interpellates around it the infinity of individuals into
> subjects in a double mirror-connexion such that it *sub-
> jects* the subjects to the Subject, while giving them in
> the Subject in which each subject can contemplate its
> own image (present and future) the *guarantee* that this
> really concerns them and Him. (1971, 180)

Althusser's references to representations of the Absolute Subject remind us of Derrida's listing of the representations of center in "Structure, Sign and Play in the Discourse of the Human Sciences": "Successively, and in a regulated fashion, the center receives different

forms or names . . . essence, existence, substance, subject . . ." (1978, 279–80). Bearing in mind the subject's incarnation as the center we remember that Derrida (1978) also says:

> it was necessary to begin thinking that there was no center, that the center could not be thought in the form of a present-being, that the center had no natural site, that it was not a fixed locus but a function, a sort of nonlocus in which an infinite number of sign-substitutions came into play. (280)

This is a position of Derrida's that has been often misunderstood. Derrida insists:

> I didn't say there was no center, that we could get along without the center. I believe that the center is a function, not a being—a reality, but a function. And this function is absolutely indispensable. The subject is absolutely indispensable. I don't destroy the subject; I situate it. (1978, 271)

And what he situates the subject in, he explains in *Positions* (1981), is difference/*différance*. Derrida's point is that there is no subject who "is agent, author, and master of *différance*." Rather, subjectivity is "inscribed in a system of *différance*":

> the subject is constituted only in being divided from itself, in becoming space, in temporizing, in deferral; . . . At the point at which the concept of *différance*, and the chain attached to it, intervenes, all the conceptual oppositions of metaphysics (signifer/signified; sensible/intelligible; writing/speech; passivity/activity; etc.)—to the extent that they ultimately refer to the presence of something present (for example, in the form of the identity of the subject who is present for all his operations, present beneath every accident or event, self-present in its

"living speech," in its enunciations, in the present objects and acts of its language, etc.)—become nonpertinent. (1981, 28–29)

My linking of quotations by Althusser and Derrida serves to reinforce the postmodern notion of how we apprehend 'meaning' as being a function of our social, cultural, historical situation as well as of our language. In this instance, I refer to how we apprehend the meaning of the subject. Belsey clarifies the relationship among ideology, language, and subjectivity:

> Because ideology has the role of constituting concrete individuals as subjects, because it is produced in the identification with the "I" of discourse, and is thus the condition of action, we cannot simply step outside it. To do so would be to refuse to act or speak, and even to make such a refusal, to say "I refuse," is to accept the condition of subjectivity. (1980, 62)

Belsey's last sentence is in reference to Saussure's suggestion that it is language which makes the idea of subjectivity possible by enabling the speaker to posit herself or himself as 'I', as the subject of a sentence. For Derrida this means that the subject "is a 'function' of language, becomes a *speaking* subject only by making its speech conform . . . to the system of the rules of language as a system of differences, or at very least by conforming to the general law of *différance*" (1982, 15). Derrida's idea of *différance* not only negates the mystifying notion of a transcendental signified—a signified which would exist independently of a signifier—it also negates the notion of a Cartesian subject (the key modernist version of the transcendental signified). Derrida's point is that we cannot conceive of a nonsignifying subjectivity, an originary consciousness.

The relationship between language and subjectivity has been further developed through Jacques Lacan's reading of Freud. Lacan adds to Freud's decentering of the rational consciousness the insights of structural linguistics. He posits the subject as constructed in lan-

guage, and as a result denies the notion of the individual consciousness as the origin of meaning and knowledge. Lacan is thus working
within the postmodern moment which decenters the individual as
transcendental signified. Within the Lacanian paradigm, the infant
has no way of perceiving her or his own identity as separate from
what is exterior to it. During the 'mirror-phase' of the child's development (at six to eight months old) it 'recognizes' itself as distinct
from the outside world. The term 'mirror-phase' refers to the awareness of the subject of itself as separate from the mother, for example.
Such a recognition does not require an actual mirror; the terminology
refers, however, to an identification with an 'imaginary' (because im-
aged) unitary and autonomous self.

The self-recognition, or identification, that takes place during the
mirror-phase is, however, alienating. In Lacan's terms:

> This jubilant assumption of his specular image by the
> child . . . would seem to exhibit in an exemplary situation
> the symbolic matrix in which the *I* is precipitated in a
> primordial form, before it is objectified in the dialectic
> of identification with the other, and before language re-
> stores to it, in the universal, its function as subject.
> (1977, 2)

This "assumption of his specular image" is alienating in that this
wholeness is seen as 'other', as a fiction. The child's behavior when
faced by his peers during this stage "will be dominated by the trap-
ping of the being by the image of the human form" (Lemaire, 1977,
80). In other words, the child recognizes him/herself as separate in
the mirror-phase, but at this phase also identifies her/himself with
equal-age peers, recognizing these peers as they replicate the image
he/she has seen in the mirror "of the human form": "the child who
strikes will say that he has been struck, the child who sees his fellow
fall will cry" (Lemaire, 1977, 80). As Anika Lemaire (1977) explains,
the reflection of the body in the mirror stage is: "salutary in that it
is unitary and localized in time and space. But the mirror stage is
also the stage of alienating narcissistic identification (primary iden-

tification); the subject *is* his own double more than he is himself" (81).

The child's movement into subjectivity, however, comes with her/his entry into language. The acquisition of language marks the entry into the symbolic order, as the child becomes a member of social formations by acknowledging and participating in society's signifying systems, most specifically, in language. This symbolic order of signs and meanings pre-exists the infant's birth. The child must enter into the symbolic order in order to become an effective member of the community. The major movement into language, and thus, subjectivity, comes as the child makes the distinction between 'you' and 'I' which is necessary in order for the child to speak intelligibly. The child's identification as 'I' thus constitutes the basis of subjectivity. The terms 'ego' or 'self' are misleading in understanding Lacan's concept of the subject, since "they imply a wholeness or totality that he refuted by his literal reformulation of the Freudian idea of a . . . splitting of the subject" (Ragland-Sullivan, 1986, 2).

Lacan's introduction of linguistics to our understanding of subjectivity has a series of ramifications, most specifically in that the self is perceived, as a result, as always radically fractured into the *speaking* subject and the subject of *being*: the subject that can *speak* his/her self-knowledge is always separated from the subject that *knows*. This splitting, and the play between the speaking subject and the subject of being should be more understandable when we remember the play of, and the gaps in which meaning takes place between, the linguistic elements of signified and signifier. Lemaire explains how the study of language leads Lacan to consider the thesis that:

> birth into language and the utilization of the symbol produce a disjunction between the lived experience and the sign which replaces it. This disjunction will become greater over the years, language being above all the organ of communication and of reflection upon a lived experience which it is often not able to go beyond. Always seeking to "rationalize," to "repress" the lived experi-

ence, reflection will eventually become profoundly di-
vergent from that lived experience. In this sense, we can
say with Lacan that the appearance of language is simultaneous with the primal repression which constitutes
the unconscious. (1977, 53)

In other words, there is no unmediated access to the innermost part
of the psyche, which is different from the subject of conscious discourse. This discourse, as part of the symbolic order "mediates" the
subject "and thus lends itself particularly well to a rapid turning
away from truth" (Lemaire, 1977, 67). As such, the symbolic order
cannot be referred directly to what Lacan calls "the real." Such a
splitting of speaking and being within the subject allows Lacan to
rephrase the famous Cartesian proclamation:

> "I am what I think," therefore I am: divide the "I am"
> of existence from the "I am" of meaning. This splitting
> must be taken as being principle, and as the first outline
> of primal repression, which, as we know, establishes the
> unconscious. (in Lemaire, 1977, 77)

But this is not to say that this splitting does not allow the subject
to form an identity of itself. The subject's identity is the image of
itself that the subject forms by identifying with others' perceptions
of it. But the child learns to say 'me' and 'I' only by acquiring these
designations from someone and somewhere else, from the world
which perceives and names it. The terms 'me' and 'I' do not develop
naturally out of the child's experience of its body or 'self'; rather,
these terms come from elsewhere.[6]

As time progresses the child learns to identify itself through a
series of subject positions (as 'boy' or 'girl', younger or older, for
example), and the child's amalgamations of subject positions come
to provide his or her 'identity', or subjectivity, even though these
positions may be inconsistent or even contradictory with each other.
Lacan's human subject is thus the obverse of the humanists': his
subject is not an entity with a unitary identity, but a being constituted

within a matrix of identities. In other words, Lacan's picture of the human subject stands in contradiction to the post-Cartesian, empirical, and pragmatic basis of most current Western thought that considers the ego to be a fixed, whole entity that is innate or instinctual.

Cathy Urwin (1984) in "Power Relations and the Emergence of Language" suggests that according to Lacan, it is only through entering into the symbolic order as a speaking subject

> that full consciousness or autonomy over the immediacy of current events is possible at all. And, in consequence, for Lacan language acquisition is the central process whereby conscious subjectivity is produced, to be continually reproduced every time we use language, whether as adults or children. (275)

As such, Lacan is consistent with, but moves beyond Saussure's proposition that language is not a function of the speaking subject, but that the subject is a function of language.

Subjectivity is often a central problematic in feminist criticism which also takes issue with the Cartesian subject.[7] A feminist critique points out the historical aspects of the gendered subject; much of feminism is a reclaiming or naming of the woman as subject. But, again, rather than be caught in an essentializing substitution ("we weren't subjects, but look at us now") feminism is more often directed toward analyses of the conditions of possibility that constitute the various roles of women in various subject positions. Because feminism often hinges on how 'woman' is denied subjectivity through the concept of the 'rational' and thus 'male' *cogito*, its critique often begins with a look back at Freudian psychoanalysis in which 'woman' is defined in terms of a 'lack' (of the penis). For some readings of Freud, the biological fact of a male having a penis constitutes the way in which the male's own identity as a male is constructed—through his anxiety about losing it (castration). This biological fact is also the means by which the female is constructed as the female, by virtue of being always-already castrated. Lacan moves the emphasis from the penis as biological determinator, to the 'Phallus' as signifier of presence, or more correctly, as the symbolic meaning of absence or lack. Lemaire explains how the Phallus, "which fills the empty space," denies lack:

> For a psychoanalysis with a firm theoretical basis, the important thing is, Lacan will say, to make it known and understood that none in fact has this mythical phallus which will exclude lack. That on the contrary, man has a penis, an organ which has been elected to the function of a "phallic" symbol of non-lack and which consequently engenders the conflicting forms of the male and female castration complexes. (1977, 59)

As a result, many contemporary feminist theorists turn to Lacan's reworking of Freud and his emphasis on signification rather than on the lack or presence of the penis. However, despite this shift from innate biological difference to the production of subjectivity in accordance with cultural laws, the phallus as the sign of difference remains, for Lacan, the 'signifier of signifieds'.

Juliet Mitchell in *Feminine Sexuality* (1982) explains:

> For all psychoanalysts the development of the human subject, its unconscious and its sexuality go hand-in-hand, they are causatively intertwined. . . . The selection of the phallus as the mark around which subjectivity and sexuality are constructed reveals, precisely, that they are constructed, in a division which is both arbitrary and alienating. In Lacan's reading of Freud, the threat of castration is not something that has been done to an already existent girl subject or that could be done to an already existent boy subject; it is, as it was for Freud, what 'makes' the girl a girl and the boy a boy, in a division that is both essential and precarious. . . . The phallus—with its status as potentially absent—comes to stand in for the necessarily *missing* object of desire at the level of sexual division. (2,7,24)

Jacqueline Rose, also in *Feminine Sexuality* (1982), states it this way:

> For Lacan, the unconscious undermines the subject from any position of certainty, from any relation of knowledge to his or her psychic processes and history, and *simultaneously* reveals the fictional nature of the sexual category to which every human subject is none the less assigned. In Lacan's account, sexual identity operates as a law—it is something enjoined on the subject. (29)

Once again the concept of the subject as 'subjected to' is introduced. And what the subject is subjected to, or within, is a system of signification, of meaning, in which the phallus acts as an ultimate signifier of cultural differences between genders.

On the one hand, a number of readers see this emphasis on the Phallus instead of the penis, and the corresponding shift from nature to culture, as a small step for man and just about as small a step for (hu)mankind because it continues to position the female as absence. In other words, although the Phallus may thus be representative of the fiction of unmediated absence, the question remains: why this particular trope? That is, the use of the term Phallus continues to reify the relation between presence/absence and male sexuality. It reproduces rather than demystifies that relation, even as it purports to demystify subjectivity itself. On the other hand, this emphasis on signification may be seen as a positive step away from a normalizing view of 'reality' in which the subject is formulated as male because the male 'has' whereas the female 'has not', and in which this formulation is considered to be ideologically neutral. Signification, as the process of making sense, is a production, rather than a neutral representation. Signification refers to the processes whereby meaning is produced at the same time as subjects are fabricated and positioned in social relations. As such, the use of the term signification incorporates and moves beyond modern structural linguistics; the argument is not simply that language determines meaning, but that those practices which constitute our everyday lives are produced and reproduced as an integral part of the production of signs and signifying systems. The processes of signification and subjectification work simultaneously and intimately; any time we speak of the subject we must also speak of the social because the subject is fabricated within signifying practices. Thus, as we saw in Chapter 2, there isn't an overarching 'reality' which determines the representation or the means of representation; instead, the process of signification itself gives shape to the reality it implicates.

This is, of course, the briefest of sketches of the Lacanian project, and refers to only a small segment of it. What is important for our purposes is that the subject is not a stable, unified pregiven entity, separate from but interacting with the world, and that how we perceive the subject is deeply imbricated in ideology. There is no unmediated experience; there is no way to gain access to some inner and pure pre-social self, because there is no such self. Rather, the subject is the site of conflict and contradiction, constructed and altered through language and social formation. And as Belsey states, "in the fact that the subject is a *process* lies the possibility of transformation" (1980, 65). It is this subject as process that we will study more closely in Michel Tournier's novel *Friday*.

PART II: *The Subject and Power*

Much of *Friday* lends itself to a discussion of subjectivity, most obviously in terms of how this particular Robinson Crusoe charts, as he sees it, his evolution. For example, we could identify how Crusoe's changing perceptions of self (as he ponders who am 'I') hearken to a particular moment in the history of the subject. For example, how is he (and where is he) the combination of the medieval 'I' believe, the Cartesian 'I' think, the Romantic 'I' feel, the existential 'I' choose, the Freudian 'I' dream, and so forth? A second, and, I believe, fruitful analysis would refer to a Journal entry of Crusoe's (Tournier, 91–95) which presents Crusoe's own attempt at a philosphy of the subject. Crusoe's philosophy appears to rely most specifically on a Kantian sense of the subject as the transcendental condition for knowing, but also moves into a more contemporary realm with his emphasis on the need for the presence of an 'other' in order to have a particular kind of knowledge. Also, Tournier's book calls out for a discussion from a feminist point of view on Crusoe's relationship with the is-land-as-woman (as virgin to be dominated and cultivated, then as mother, then as wife, and finally as something earthly to be su-perceded by a more mature and fulfilling solar relationship).[8] Or we could study Althusser's connection between ideology and subjectivity in terms of Crusoe's replication and installation of the apparatuses of state, religion, and the military on his island (see Chapter 4). Each of these projects would open Tournier's text for further study of subjectivity.

Another option, which I pursue in detail here, is to note how subjectivity in *Friday* has been formulated in terms of Michel Fou-cault's discussion of the subject in relation to power. In the remainder of this chapter I present passages from Foucault's 1982 essay "The Subject and Power" in conjunction with passages from Tournier's novel Friday[9] (for the most part limited to Chapter 8). Both Foucault's essay and this specific section of *Friday*, I suggest, provide a com-mentary on the relationship between power and subjectivity. I use the essay as a means by which to comment on the novel and the novel as a means by which to clarify the essay. Ultimately, the purpose here is to privilege neither the essay nor the novel, but rather, by reading the two together, to understand more fully the position of subjectivity within a power relationship.

In "The Subject and Power" Foucault states that the goal of his work during the preceding twenty years has been to create a "history of the different modes by which, in our culture, human beings are made subjects" (1982, 777). In *The Order of Things* Foucault pro-vided an archaeology of contemporary discourses in Western civili-zation in the past approximately five hundred years. Foucault's proj-ect was

> to explore scientific discourse not from the point of view
> of the individuals who are speaking, nor from the point
> of view of the formal structures of what they are saying,

> but from the point of view of the rules that come into
> play in the very existence of such discourse: what con-
> ditions did [theorists] have to fulfil, not to make [their]
> discourse coherent and true in general, but to give it, at
> the time when it was written and accepted, value and
> practical application as scientific discourse. (1982, xiv)

Discourse refers to a regulated system of statements which can be
analyzed not solely in terms of its internal rules of formation, but
also as a set of practices within a social milieu. Discourse is the
combination of a practice and a mode or structure of speaking. Foucault points out that a discourse itself furnishes the very criteria by
which its results are judged successful. In *The Order of Things* Foucault's archaeology of knowledge—an attempt to look at historical
periods from their own perspective on knowledge and language rather
than from a teleological point of view in which all history is made
sense of through current paradigms—is presented in terms of "epistemes," paradigms or social *a prioris* that constitute "the very
ground upon which truth and falsity can be debated" (Harland, 1987,
105).

Foucault presents the four major epistemes of the last five centuries: Renaissance, Classical, Modern, and Post-Modern cum Structuralist (the latter of which is still in the process of arriving). In the
Renaissance period

> the division between the human and the non-human
> does not exist. . . . What we now see as the natural world
> appears in the Renaissance as a great artifice, a great
> book, in which God, as the word itself, inscribes signs
> and clues and an endless play of overlapping resem-
> blances for men to interpret. (Harland, 1987, 109)

With the early seventeenth-century Classical episteme the non-human splits off from the human: "the natural world becomes an object
to be known by the human mind as a subject." This way of knowing
is representation: "the mind re-presents a simulacrum of the outside

world" (Harland, 1987, 110). The focus becomes visible and thus nameable and classifiable in nature. Around the end of the eighteenth century, with the Modern episteme, the project becomes one of abstracting forces outside of man's direct experience. For example, in the natural sciences the emphasis is no longer on the interaction of substantial bodies, but on concepts such as electricity, heat, magnetism; in economics, the emphasis shifts from the movement of substantial goods to what appears to be the underlying and 'hidden' history of the goods: the human labor expended in the production of these goods. The result of this notion of abstract forces in all aspects of experience is that the Classical dichotomy between the subject as mirror and the object as referent becomes irrelevant: the same abstract forces run through both the human subject and non-human object.

More to the point of subjectivity, however, is Foucault's assertion that the appearance of "man" takes place during this Modern episteme, that man, as we think of the subject, is only about two hundred years old.[10] What Foucault is referring to is the establishment of the specifically *human* sciences (anthropology, sociology, psychology) in which the human subject is now constituted on the side of the object. That is, man becomes both the object of study *and* the subject that studies, the object of knowledge and the subject who knows. This is the concept of the subject that we are most familiar with, indeed, the one we take for granted. Foucault suggests that (with the still-arriving Post-Modern episteme) man is in the process of disappearing again, as Freudian psychoanalysis and Saussurean linguistics, for example, indicate a new abstract force of signs and signification not reckoned for or tolerated by the positivistic approach available in the Modern episteme. As the dichotomy between subject and object begins to fail, man's sense of superiority and mastery in his capacity to know and be known evaporates.

In later work Foucault moves from a project of archaeology to genealogy. Richard Harland explains that the "most obvious aspect of the difference between 'archaeology' and 'genealogy' is that the latter puts the emphasis on power rather than upon knowledge, upon practices rather than upon language" (1987, 155). Foucault's essay

"The Subject and Power" is thus a genealogical study with reference to his archaeological work on man as the object of knowledge and the subject who knows. In this essay Foucault lists three modes of "objectification," that is, the means by which human beings are transformed into subjects. First are the modes of inquiry which try to give themselves the status of sciences: for example, the objectivizing of the speaking subject in philology or linguistics, or of the productive subject (as the subject who labors) in the analysis of wealth. Second is the objectivizing of the subject in "dividing practices" in which the subject is either divided in himself or divided from others (as mad or sane, sick or healthy, for example). The third mode is the way a human being turns himself into a subject of an abstract field of experience. Foucault gives the example of how men have learned to recognize themselves as subjects of "sexuality."

Foucault suggests that although the subject is placed in relations of production (Althusser) and of signification (Derrida, Kristeva, Barthes, Lacan, for example), he equally is placed in complex power relations. Foucault states that in order to develop a theory of power relations we need to investigate the links between rationalization (referring to underlying, accepted principles of meaning and understanding) and power, and to do this we need to analyze separate fields, each with reference to a fundamental experience: for example, madness, illness, death, crime, sexuality, and so forth. The word 'rationalization', Foucault cautions, is dangerous; we need to analyze specific rationalities. His caution should be familiar to us at this point: it is first a reminder against accepting terms as metaphysical absolutes that remain unchanged across time and circumstance; it is second (and this is of course related) an insistence on the historic specificity of each area of rationality.

Another way to work toward an understanding of power relations would be to use forms of resistance taken against different forms of power as a means by which to bring to light power relations, locate their position, and find out their points of application and methods used—that is, to analyze "power relations through the antagonism of strategies." For example, says Foucault, "to find out what our society means by sanity, perhaps we should investigate what is happening in the field of insanity" (1982, 780). Rather than talk about power in terms of who makes decisions, or who controls whom, perhaps we should investigate the forms of resistance and the attempts made to dislocate and dissociate power relations.

For our purposes, we will look at the relationship in Tournier's *Friday* between Robinson Crusoe and Friday to analyze the subjectivity/power nexus in light of forms of resistance. That is, we will look at their power relationship in light of Friday's resistance to Crusoe's government (regardless of the degree to which that resistance is presented as following a consistent or predetermined pattern). Friday's resistance may be seen as that moment which locates the position of power relations, their point of application, and methods used. In short, I will be using the moment in *Friday* (restricted, I suggest, to Chapter 8) at which there is an active relation of power between the two individuals as the fictional focus for this discussion on the subject and power.

Well over half of Tournier's novel takes place with only Crusoe on the island, before Friday appears and is mistakenly saved from death by Crusoe. (Crusoe means to shoot Friday but is bumped by his dog and shoots Friday's pursuer instead.) As a result:

> a naked and panic-stricken black man pressed his forehead to the ground, while with one hand he groped for the foot of a bearded and armed white man, clad in goatskin and a bonnet of fur, accoutered with the trappings of three thousand years of Western civilization, and sought to place it on his neck. (Tournier, 135)

This moment of submission occurs in Chapter 7, and for some time thereafter Friday is docile and obedient. Chapter 8 begins with Friday waking one morning to find Crusoe gone and the water-clock stopped. With Crusoe's ordered system in suspension, Friday becomes "his own master and master of the island" (Tournier, 149) and sets forth on what appears to be a capricious, but effective, program of disruption to Crusoe's island orderliness. First Friday hauls a chest of rich fabrics and jewels (which Crusoe had secured from the ship) to a part of the island covered by sand dunes and cacti. There he dresses and bedecks the cacti until he has before him a series of vegetable mannequins. Then he moves off, "drunk with his own youth and freedom in that boundless place where every movement was possible and nothing could cut off his vision" (Tournier, 152). In the process of skimming stones, Friday sends a stone into the rice paddy which, as a symbol of hard work, ingenuity, and control over nature, was a source of both concern and satisfaction for Crusoe. The dog chases the stone into the paddy and is quickly stuck in the too-shallow-to-swim-in but too-muddy-to-get-out-of water. Friday quickly responds to the dog's danger by raising the sluice gate, thus draining the paddy and ruining the rice crop. To Friday,

> the stopping of the clock and the absence of Robinson were two aspects of a single event, a break in the established order. To Robinson, Friday's disappearance, the dressing of the cacti, and the drying out of the rice paddy all pointed to the inadequacy and perhaps total failure of his attempts to domesticate the Araucanian. It was rare, in any case, for Friday to do anything of his own accord that did not displease Robinson. He could only escape rebuke by meticulously following instructions, or by doing nothing. Robinson had been obliged to recognize that beneath the show of submissiveness, Friday possessed a mind of his own, and that what came out of it was profoundly shocking and subversive of discipline on the island. (Tournier, 154)

Friday is on his own for a few more days during which he replants shrubbery upside down and finally allows himself to be discovered in the disguise of a human plant. From that time on Friday is back with Crusoe, but causing his "master" increasing concern:

> Not merely did [Friday] fail to fit harmoniously into the system, but an alien presence, he even threatened to destroy it. . . . [W]ith every appearance of good will, he

was proving himself utterly unreceptive to principles of order and organization, planning and husbandry. (Tournier, 156)

At the same time, Crusoe finds himself questioning his own systematic way of life in light of Friday's actions. When Friday feeds an orphaned fledgling vulture by chewing grubs that appeared on rotting goat intestines and then dribbling "the white unspeakable pap" into the vulture's open beak, Crusoe flees with his stomach heaving. But,

> [f]or the first time he questioned his white man's sensibilities, his queasy fastidiousness, wondering if this were a last rare token of civilization, or only dead weight that he must be willing to shed before embarking upon a new way of life. (Tournier, 163–64)

Nevertheless, "the Governor, the General, and the Pastor" still hold the upper hand in Crusoe, and the "sum of his grievances" against Friday ultimately comes to rest on his fear that Friday also knows "the secret of the pink coomb." For some time Speranza, Crusoe's name for his island, had been the "island-wife" of Crusoe, who believed that having sex with the earth in a particular meadow was resulting in the creation of mandrake plants: "It was true! His love-making with Speranza was not sterile. The white, fleshy, curiously forked root bore an undeniable resemblance of the body of a woman-child" (Tournier, 129). When Crusoe discovers Friday repeating Crusoe's act in the meadow, he is "thunderstruck, contemplating the infamy taking place beneath his eyes. Speranza sullied, outraged by a Negro!" (Tournier, 167). Seeing himself in specifically Jehovah-like images, Crusoe beats Friday severely, and then guiltily beats a hasty retreat back to read the Bible. A passage in the Book of Hosea allows him to shift the blame onto Speranza, the adulterous woman-earth. At this point Crusoe feels he is quickly approaching some change and watches Friday: "For the first time he was clearly envisaging the possibility that within that crude and brutish half-caste who so exasperated him another Friday might be concealed" (Tournier, 172). Crusoe, however, dismisses the thought and returns once more to his daily regimen.

The final blow to Crusoe's orderly empire is cataclysmic, certain, and brought to bear by Friday. Friday had discovered Crusoe's pipe and one jar of hoarded tobacco and was fascinated by the rising eddy of smoke from the pipe. Upon Crusoe's absence one day Friday took the tobacco and pipe into the supply cave to smoke. When the angry Crusoe returned before expected, Friday in fright threw the pipe well back into the cave toward the kegs of gun powder stored there by Crusoe. Chapter 8 ends with the explosion that brings down Crusoe's empire.

The next chapter begins by detailing the destruction:

> The Residence was burning like a torch. The crenelated wall of the fortress had collapsed into the moat. The office building, the Meeting Hall, and the calendar mast, being lighter, had been blown to bits. (Tournier, 177)

To Crusoe it seemed "that Friday had triumphed at last over the state of affairs he so detested" (Tournier, 179). From that point on, passive and waiting, Crusoe follows Friday. And thus, in Foucault's terms, as we shall see, active power *relations* have ended. (We shall also see that Foucault's prose is not readily paraphrased, and thus, in the following discussion on power relations and subjectivity I will be presenting longish passages from "The Subject and Power" followed by readings of *Friday*.)

Foucault suggests that a starting point in analyzing power relations may be to look at series of oppositions, such as opposition to the power of men over women, of psychiatry over the mentally ill, or of administration over the ways people live, and to identify what they have in common. What they share is that the

> aim of these struggles is the power effects as such. For example, the medical profession is not criticized primarily because it is a profit-making concern but because

> it exercises an uncontrolled power over people's bodies, their health, and their life and death. (Foucault, 1982, 780)

That is to say, resistance is not focused on the abstract and encompassing body of the more powerful structure, but rather, on the immediate effects of that structure's power. Thus, the struggles are focused on the effects of power on the individual body. These resistances are also

> struggles which question the status of the individual: on the one hand, they assert the right to be different, and they underline everything which makes individuals truly individual. On the other hand, they attack everything which separates the individual, breaks his links with others, splits up community life, forces the individual back on himself, and ties him to his own identity in a constraining way.
>
> These struggles are not exactly for or against the "individual" but rather they are struggles against the "government of individualization." (1982, 781)

How does the statement "the aim of these struggles is the power effects as such" translate in *Friday*? Friday does not resist Crusoe's government because he wishes to undo Crusoe's structures and order; he bears no real malice toward Crusoe's regimen. Friday's resistance is to that which he finds physically encumbering, to that which restrains his body. Friday's dream is based on flight: "If only he could fly! If he could turn himself into a butterfly!" (Tournier, 152). Thus, it is not unusual that Friday's disruptive actions would take the form of flights of fancy that turn Crusoe's world of order and restraint upside down.

Foucault's suggestion that the oppositions in power relations are "struggles which question the status of the individual" is complex. When he says that these struggles "assert the right to be different" he is suggesting the not-too-surprising impulse for women, for example, to insist that they not only have equal rights, responsibilities, roles, that is, 'subjectivity', in this world as men, but also that they have the right not to *be* men. Or, for example, that children have a right to be different from parents. At the same time, when Foucault says that these resistances against authority attack everything which separates the individual and breaks his links with others he is suggesting that the individual attacks that which threatens not just his individuality but also his sense of community. This is because the community takes a determining part in how that individual is identified. For example, an individual who is a woman occupies an infinite number of subject positions (mother, union member, mechanic, friend, cat-lover, employer, etc.), but the opposition of women to the power of men over them "forces the individual back on [her]self, and ties [her] to [her] own identity in a constraining way," that is, to her identity specifically as 'woman'. This is not to say that a woman always finds her identity as a woman constraining, but rather, that the power of men over women which forces a particular identity on women, and which thus results in resistance, also restricts and constrains how women identify themselves *within* that particular struggle. Thus, this struggle "questions the status of the individual" not in that it is for or against the individual, but in that it works against the "government of individualization," that is, control, by tying the individual to a particular, and thus, restricting identity.

Now this is not an easy concept to discuss in *Friday*, mostly because although we can read the text in terms of the governor and the governed, we are given two individuals and not two opposing communities. Nonetheless, Crusoe's governorship is a replica, to his mind, of British (or Western) civilization (which means a society under the authority of Governor, Commander-in-Chief, and Pastor). Also, to Crusoe's mind, Friday represents that which is to be colonized, the slave. This is clear from the first journal entry that Crusoe writes after Friday enters the island life:

> God has sent me a companion, but through some obscure whim of Divine Wisdom, He has elected to choose one from the lowest stratum of humanity. Not only is

the man colored, a coastal Araucanian, but he is clearly
not of pure blood. Everything about him points to the
half-caste, a South American Indian crossed with Negro. . . . [A] companionship has now been bestowed on
me in its most primitive and rudimentary form, but this
will at least make it easier for me to mold it to my
requirements. My course is clear. I must fit my slave into
the system which I have perfected over the years. (Tournier, 138–39)

The "government of individualization" is clearly oppressive here: Friday's subject position is named by Crusoe. Indeed, the role of naming
is crucial. Crusoe writes:

I had to find a name for the newcomer. I did not choose
to give him a Christian name until he was worthy of
that dignity. A savage is not wholly a human being. . . .
I think I have solved the problem with some elegance in
giving him the name of the day on which I saved him—
Friday. It is the name neither of a person nor of a common
object, but somewhat between the two, that of a half-
living, half-abstract entity. (Tournier, 139)

Thus, when Friday resists, it will be not so much against Crusoe, as
against the restrictions he feels as a result of Crusoe's view of Friday's
subject position, against being forced into his Crusoe-given, and thus
singular, identity. Friday's is a struggle against "the government of
individualization."

Foucault also posits an opposition to the effects of power which
are struggles against the privileges of knowledge. These struggles:

are an opposition to the effects of power which are linked
with knowledge, competence, and qualification: struggles against the privileges of knowledge. But they are
also an opposition against secrecy, deformation, and
mystifying representations imposed on people.

... What is questioned is the way in which knowledge circulates and functions, its relations to power. ....
    Finally, all these present struggles revolve around the
question: Who are we? They are a refusal of these ab-
stractions, of economic and ideological state violence,
which ignore who we are individually, and also a refusal
of a scientific or administrative inquisition which determines who one is. (1982, 781)

For Foucault, knowledge is an integral piece to the power/subjectivity
nexus. A will to knowledge is a will to power. Crusoe's authority,
again within his structured island, is partly as the representative of
British civilization, but even more so as the spokesman for the authority of the Bible. As the holder and interpreter of the Bible as
ultimate truth, Crusoe bears the privilege of knowledge. We shouldn't
be surprised then to see early indications of Friday's opposition, un-
planned but uncanny, played out in the form of resistance to ultimate
truth:

> Friday was required to repeat after [Crusoe] the religious
> and moral axioms which [Crusoe] propounded in mea-
> sured tones. For example—"God is an all-powerful, om-
> niscient master, infinitely good, merciful and just, the
> Creator of Man and of All Things." And Friday's laugh
> rang out irrepressible, lyrical, and blasphemous, to be
> extinguished like a snuffed candle by a resounding blow
> on the cheek. (Tournier, 140)

Foucault sums up the section on resistance by tying together the
notion of "government of individualization" and "subjectivization,"
saying that

> the main objective of these struggles is to attack not so
> much "such or such" an institution of power, or group,
> or elite, or class but rather a technique, a form of power.

This form of power applies itself to immediate everyday life which categorizes the individual, marks him out by his own individuality, attaches him to his own identity, imposes a law of truth on him which he must recognize and which others have to recognize in him. It is a form of power which makes individuals subjects. There are two meanings of the word "subject": subject to someone else by control and dependence; and tied to his own identity by a conscience or self-knowledge. Both meanings suggest a form of power which subjugates and makes subject to. (1982, 781)

Within the novel *Friday*, Crusoe categorizes Friday as the subordinate, as the slave, and does so by shaping his daily life, by fitting him within a system that is neither of Friday's shaping nor is sensible within his frame of reference. Thus, Friday understands his role or identity within Crusoe's system:

All that his master ordered was right, all that he forbade was wrong. It was good to toil night and day for the functioning of an elaborate system that served no purpose; it was bad to eat more than the portion allotted to him by his master. It was good to be a soldier when his master was a general, a choir-boy when his master prayed, a builder's laborer when he built, a farm laborer when he farmed, a herdsman when he herded, a beater when he hunted, a paddler when he traveled by water, a bedside attendant when he was sick, an operator of the fan, and a killer of flies. It was wrong to smoke a pipe, to go naked, or to hide when there was work to be done. (Tournier, 140)

Thus, by identifying himself according to Crusoe's "law of truth," the 'individual' Friday becomes the subject Friday. He is subject to Crusoe's control and while subject to this control is known to himself as his master's slave.

Foucault suggests that currently one type of struggle is becoming increasingly important: the struggle "against that which ties the individual to himself and submits him to others in this way" (1982, 781). Foucault calls this a struggle against the forms of subjection, against the submission of subjectivity, and says that this kind of struggle prevails in our society because of the political structure known as the "state." And although the state is often thought of as a kind of political power

> which ignores individuals, looking only at the interests of the totality or, I should say, of a class or a group among the citizens. . . . the state's power (and that's one of the reasons for its strength) is both an individualizing and a totalizing form of power. (Foucault, 1982, 782)

Foucault, whose work often moves beyond analysis to advocacy, suggests that

> We have to imagine and to build up what we could be to get rid of this kind of political "double bind," which is the simultaneous individualization and totalization of modern power structures.
>
> The conclusion would be that the political, ethical, social, philosophical problem of our days is not to try to liberate the individual from the state and from the state's institutions but to liberate us both from the state and from the type of individualization which is linked to the state. We have to promote new forms of subjectivity through the refusal of this kind of individuality which has been imposed on us for several centuries. (1982, 785)

In other words, the power of the state is most visible in its relation to totalities (classes or groups), but this power not only totalizes, but also, and more to the point, individualizes. It individualizes in the sense described above in that it ties the individual to a particular identity, thus leading to the submission of subjectivity. Foucault says that in order to get out of this political double bind of a simultaneous individualization and totalization, that is, to liberate ourselves from the type of individualization linked to the state, we need to refuse this kind of individuality.

Foucault links this combination of individualization techniques and totalization procedures of the Western state to a power technique which originated in Christian institutions; he calls this power technique "pastoral" power. Pastoral power is salvation-oriented and "linked with a production of truth—the truth of the individual himself" (1982, 783). Foucault sees the modern state as continuing a new form of pastoral power. As such, the "modern state" is not

> an entity which was developed above individuals, ignoring what they are and even their very existence, but, on the contrary, [is] a very sophisticated structure, in which individuals can be integrated, under one condition: that this individuality would be shaped in a new form and subjected to a set of very specific patterns. (1982, 783)

Tournier's Robinson Crusoe quite explicitly represents the state: in his first encounter with Friday he is pictured as "accoutered with the trappings of three thousand years of Western civilization" (Tournier, 135). Crusoe sets up a Charter of the Island of Speranza as well as a Penal Code. He builds a Conservatory of Weights and Measures, a Meeting Hall for worship, and a fortress. He is Governor, Pastor, General. Representing the state in the analogy I am presenting here, Crusoe's position is not that of a disinterested power totally above and ignoring Friday. Rather, Crusoe's structure demands that Friday be integrated within it, that Friday as individual be reshaped and submitted to Crusoe's very specific cultural and pastoral structure:

> Thus, during the first weeks after Friday's arrival, the administration of the island once again became Robinson's main preoccupation, as he fulfilled his roles of Governor, Commander in Chief, and Spiritual Pastor. For a

while he even believed that the newcomer would provide
a justification for his structure, a weight and stability
that would finally do away with the dangers threatening
him, just as some ships are not fully seaworthy until
ballasted with a certain amount of cargo. (Tournier, 144)

Now for Friday to refuse the kind of subjectivity imposed on
him by Crusoe would be to not fit into Crusoe's production of truth.
That is, if Crusoe's system of governorship is based on a truth, then
the newcomer Friday, as slave, should fit smoothly into Crusoe's structure. In fact, in light of Crusoe's endeavors, for years all his island
lacked was the individual represented by Friday, the 'native' to be
colonized. But Friday resists this individualization by the state by not
fitting in, by remaining an 'other', outside of the truth of Crusoe's
order. The best example of how Friday is within, while without,
Crusoe's structure is the hole-digging episode. Crusoe is, of course,
disconcerted by Friday's seeming inability to fit into a 'civilized' structure. That is, Friday obeys orders, but does so in a way that makes
clear that he recognizes no logic, or truth, to Crusoe's system. Crusoe
writes in his journal:

> Weary of watching him obey my orders mechanically,
> without showing any interest in the reason for them, I
> resolved to carry the matter to its logical conclusion. I
> set him a task which in every prison in the world is held
> to be the most degrading of harassments—the task of
> digging a hole and filling it in with the contents of a
> second; then digging a third, and so on. He labored at
> this for an entire day, under a leaden sky and in heat like
> that of a furnace. . . . To say that Friday gave no sign of
> resenting this idiotic employment is not enough. I have
> seldom seen him work with such good will. He did so,
> indeed, with a kind of enthusiasm which seems to refute
> the two alternative theories I had applied to him—either
> that he is utterly dull-witted, or that he believes me to
> be mad. I have to look elsewhere . . . (Tournier, 146)

Crusoe's comparison of his actions over Friday to a prison-like task brings us to Foucault's assertion that it is necessary to distinguish between power that "stems from aptitudes directly inherent in the body or relayed by external instruments" from power which "brings into play relations between individuals (or between groups)" (1982, 786). The former "power" is more appropriately referred to as "capacity": the ability to modify, use, consume or destroy. It is the capacity to act upon another. The term "power," however, designates *relationships*.[11] The exercise of power itself, says Foucault,

> is a way in which certain actions modify others. Which is to say, of course, that something called Power, with or without a capital letter, which is assumed to exist universally in a concentrated or diffused form, does not exist. Power exists only when it is put into action. (1982, 788)

There are two crucial points here. The first is that the exercise of power is evidenced in actions modifying other actions, and thus is an exercise of relationship. The second is that power is not to be seen as something with an origin or a basic nature: it is denied the position of a transcendental signified.

Foucault is completely within the postmodern moment when he suggests that in order to study power we must look at it relationally: what happens in the process of power being exerted by one individual over another? When he speaks of power as a question of capacity he refers to the power Crusoe has over Friday in terms of, for example, physical strength. But more to Foucault's point is power as that which connects individuals. Without at least two individuals or factions or groups there can be no such thing as power. It is not an absolute entity; it only exists relationally. To speak of power, then, is to ask "What happens when individuals exert (as they say) power over others?" (Foucault, 1982, 786).

Power is not a thing; it is an exchange, a moment; it exists only in action, in between, in struggle. Perhaps it is useful to think of power in many of the same terms used to understand *différance*, not as a thing, but as a location of relationship. If power is not a thing, it is

> not a function of consent. In itself it is not a renunciation of freedom, a transference of rights, the power of each and all ·delegated to a few (which does not prevent the possibility that consent may be a condition for the existence or the maintenance of power). . . . In effect, what defines a relationship of power is that it is a mode of action which does not act directly and immediately on others. Instead, it acts upon their actions: an action upon an action, on existing actions or on those which may arise in the present or the future. (Foucault, 1982, 788–89)

Foucault distinguishes power from violence which acts upon a body or upon things; violence forces, it bends, it breaks on the wheel, it destroys, or it closes the door on all possibilities. The only opposite of violence is passivity: "even though consensus and violence are the instruments or the results, they do not constitute the principle or the basic nature of power" (1982, 789). A power relationship, on the other hand, can only be articulated on the basis of two elements which are each indispensable. First, 'the other' (the one over whom power is exercised) must be thoroughly recognized and maintained to the very end as a person who acts, who is not already determined as passive or void of agency. Secondly, and as a result, within a relationship of power a whole field of responses, reactions, results, and possible inventions may open up. That is why we cannot think of power as something 'above' society, a supplementary structure that could possibly be done away with. Power relations are "rooted deep in the social nexus. . . . A society without power relations can only be an abstraction" (Foucault, 1982, 791). This isn't to say that because there can't be a society without power relations that those that are established are necessary. Instead Foucault would say that the analysis and elaboration of power relations and of freedom is a permanent political task inherent in all social existence. Thus, the exercise of power is

> always a way of acting upon an acting subject or acting subjects by virtue of their acting or being capable of action. A set of actions upon other actions. . . .
>
> When one defines the exercise of power as a mode of action upon the actions of others, when one characterizes these actions by the government of men by other men ["To govern . . . is to structure the possible field of action of others"] one includes an important element: freedom. Power is exercised only over free subjects, and only insofar as they are free. By this we mean individual or collective subjects who are faced with a field of possibilities in which several ways of behaving, several reactions and diverse comportments, may be realized. Where the determining factors saturate the whole, there is no relationship of power; slavery is not a power relationship when man is in chains. (In this case it is a question of a physical relationship of constraint.) Consequently, there is no face-to-face confrontation of power and freedom, which are mutually exclusive (freedom disappears everywhere power is exercised), but a much more complicated interplay. In this game freedom may well appear as the condition for the exercise of power (at the same time its precondition, since freedom must exist for power to be exerted, and also its permanent support, since without the possibility of recalcitrance, power would be equivalent to a physical determination). (Foucault, 1982, 789–90)

Thus, only in Chapter 8 is a power relationship possible in *Friday*. If 'the other' (the one over whom power is exercised) must be recognized as a person who acts, not until Friday seizes the day, when Crusoe absents himself and the clock stops, can there be more than a master-slave, violence-passivity relationship.

To say that a master-slave relationship is not a relationship of power will seem at first like a complete travesty. But Foucault's point is that in such a relationship, in which one side is not capable of action, and is thus not an acting subject, then the power displayed is a matter of "capacity" or constraint. In order for power relations to exist there must be "points of insubordination which, by definition, are means of escape" (1982, 794). Perhaps this distinction is most clear when we look at it as compatible with the postmodern moment. A power relationship which may only be defined relationally, which is identified as the potential for exchange, resists closure. This is why Foucault says that every relationship of power may also be discussed as a strategy of struggle:

> every strategy of confrontation dreams of becoming a relationship of power, and every relationship of power leans toward the idea that, if it follows its own line of development and comes up against direct confrontation, it may become the winning strategy. (1982, 794)

The situation in a relationship of power may never be spoken of in terms of absolutes, because it takes place in movement. That is, there is always an element of 'play' between power and freedom: "between a relationship of power and a strategy of struggle there is a reciprocal appeal, a perpetual linking and a perpetual reversal" (Foucault, 1982, 794).

But, I repeat, freedom (and thus a relationship of power) is only possible where there are acting subjects. When Friday first is 'saved' he does not meet the requirements needed to make a power relationship possible:

> Friday was utterly docile. The truth is that his spirit had died at the moment when the witch doctress pointed her finger at him, and what had fled for safety was a body without a soul. . . . Since then Friday had belonged body and soul to the white man. All that his master ordered

was right, all that he forbade was wrong. (Tournier, 139–40)

The relationship is here one of Crusoe's violence to Friday's passivity. Only with Friday's 'insubordination' on the day the clock is stopped does he become an acting subject and thus initiates the power relationship of Chapter 8. As Foucault states: "It would not be possible for power relations to exist without points of insubordination which, by definition, are means of escape" (1982, 794). Then, at the end of Chapter 8, following the explosion on the island, the structure of this particular power relationship begins to shift:

> It seemed, then, that Friday had triumphed at last over the state of affairs he so detested. . . . Unwittingly but inexorably Friday had paved the way for, and finally achieved, a cataclysm that heralded the coming of a new era (Tournier, 179)

And, as the great cedar, loosened by the explosion, falls and Friday pulls Crusoe out of the way, elements for an active power relationship are no longer available. For now, temporarily at least, Crusoe no longer sees himself as an acting subject:

> This latest blow to the earthly being of Speranza, following the destruction of the cave, broke the last bond uniting Robinson to the life he had lived before. Henceforward he was a wanderer, foot-loose and timorous, in the sole company of Friday. He would never again let go the hand that had reached down to save him on the night the tree fell. (Tournier, 181)

Crusoe is now as passive as Friday had been earlier. But for a short time, before the explosion and after the stopping of the clock, all the elements are available for a relationship of power: each individual is recognized as an acting subject and as a result a whole field of responses and reactions opens up. This exchange of position between Crusoe and Friday exemplifies the nexus of power and strategy:

> [I]f it is true that at the heart of power relations and as a permanent condition of their existence there is an insubordination and a certain essential obstinacy on the part of the principles of freedom, then there is no relationship of power without the means of escape or possible flight. Every power relationship implies, at least *in potentia*, a strategy of struggle, in which the two forces are not superimposed, do not lose their specific nature, or do not finally become confused. Each constitutes for the other a kind of permanent limit, a point of possible reversal. A relationship of confrontation reaches its term, its final moment (and the victory of one of the two adversaries), when stable mechanisms replace the freeplay of antagonistic reactions. (Foucault, 1982, 794)

This is precisely the moment reached when Crusoe vows to "never again let go the hand that had reached down to save him on the night the tree fell" (Tournier, 181). No longer adversary, Crusoe now recognizes himself within a new subject position, and calls Friday his "brother."

4

From Work to Text
to Intertextuality:
Robinson Crusoe, Foe, Friday

The author is a modern figure, a product of our society insofar as, emerging from the Middle Ages with English empiricism, French rationalism and the personal faith of the Reformation, it discovered the prestige of the individual, of, as it is more nobly put, the "human person." (Barthes, 1968, 142–43)

With this sentence Roland Barthes in his essay "The Death of the Author" suggests how the humanist perception of the subject is traditionally re-presented by the role of the author: the individual who gives life to and nourishes the work. Barthes counters, however, with what is by now a familiar critique: "it is language which speaks, not the author" (1968, 143). Barthes as structuralist ties this critique of subjectivity to what he perceives as a shift of power and authority from the author/owner to the writing itself (and then to the reader, Barthes concludes in this essay). The resulting emphasis on writing and reading as production necessarily leads to a critique of the 'work' as that entity complete in itself, whole, and encapsulating a meaning that transcends time and history. Rather, writing becomes 'text'. In beginning to define 'text', Barthes provides a fine working definition of intertextuality:

> We know that a text is not a line of words releasing a single "theological" meaning (the "message" of the Author-God) but a multi-dimensional space in which a variety of writings, none of them original, blend and clash. The text is a tissue of quotations drawn from the innumerable centres of culture. (1968, 146)

Derrida, too, in a discussion of *écriture*/writing, denies single theological meaning when he says: "The specificity of writing [is thus] intimately bound to the absence of the Father" (1981, 77). Derrida's point is that there is no such thing as a sovereign subject of *écriture*; rather, there is a system of relations between the psyche, society, the world, and so forth. This system of interrelationships is intertextuality: the multiple writings—cultural, literary, historical, psychological—that come together at any 'moment' in a particular text. In the following discussion I use Barthes's essay "From Work to Text" in conjunction with two novels, *Foe* and *Friday*, to illustrate, first, the move from work to text, and second, aspects of intertextuality.

Barthes introduces his essay by equating the work with Newtonian science, and the text with Einsteinian science. That is, the work is read within a logic of representation in which, ultimately, we can speak of something as absolute, identifiable, autonomous. But, as Barthes explains,

> Just as Einsteinian science demands that *the relativity of the frames of reference* be included in the object studied, so the combined action of Marxism, Freudianism and structuralism demands, in literature, the relativization of the relations of writer, reader and observer (critic). (1971, 156)

We have learned, of course, that the insights of poststructuralism further destabilize the concepts of the "writer, reader and observer,"

insisting that we take into consideration the inexhaustible permutations and combinations of, for example, the cultural, historical,
psychological baggage of these subject positions, and their relations
of power as well. Nonetheless, Barthes's essay provides a useful entry
into the world of the text.

Barthes initially posits the difference between the work and the
text within the framework of 'method': "the work is a fragment of
substance, occupying a part of the space of books (in a library, for
example), the Text is a methodological field" (1971, 156–57). We
may think of the difference between work and Text in terms of the
difference between product and process. The work can be displayed
("in bookshops, in catalogues, in exam syllabuses"), is to be deciphered, can be held in the hand. The Text is in motion: it is "a process
of demonstration," "exists in the movement of a discourse," is "experienced only in an activity of production" (1971, 157). Although
Barthes tells us that it would be futile to try to separate out materially
works from texts, we can use some examples as approximations here:
Daniel Defoe's 1719 'classic' *Robinson Crusoe* is read as a work,
whereas J.M. Coetzee's *Foe*, I suggest, may be read as a Text. And
although Michel Tournier's *Friday* comes to rest most comfortably
in the domain of the work, I suggest that by definition each of these
novels must be a network of texts. Poststructuralists have warned us
away from 'either/or' logic ("This is either a work or a Text!"), and
we will do well to refrain from too rigorously insisting on boundaries.
Barthes makes this point when he says that

> the Text does not stop at (good) Literature; it cannot be
> contained in a hierarchy, even in simple division of gen-
> res. What constitutes the Text is, on the contrary (or
> precisely), its subversive force in respect of the old clas-
> sifications. (1971, 157)

Think, for example, of the 'ending' of *Foe*, with its sudden narratorial
displacement in the form of an unexplained intrusion of a narrator
from outside the book's ontology, to be followed by a second tremor
two pages later, in which the intruder appears once more, 300 years

after the novel's time frame, yet within it. *Foe* is in this sense a Text "which goes to the limit of the rules of enunciation (rationality, readability, etc.)" (1971, 157). That the text is perceived as unreadable is precisely one of its points, for it is 'unreadable' only according to a particular set of expectations concerning the work. To disrupt these expectations and to call attention to the very specific cultural and historical assumptions behind these expectations is part of the Text's agenda.

Foe disrupts the expectations of representation on several levels, but once again, most notably in its last five pages. Part IV is presented from the point of view of a narrator who is not only not part of the cast of characters thus far, but is also outside the story itself. This narrator enters Foe's room to find, evidently, Foe and Barton dead. The narrator then lies on the floor beside Friday: "From his mouth, without a breath, issue the sounds of the island" (Coetzee, 154). At this point, the text is interrupted, and the narrator once again enters the house, but this time notes a plaque bolted to the wall which reads *Daniel Defoe, Author*, intimating that we are now entering, with the narrator, an altogether different level of ontology.[1] Our narrator tells us that the room "is darker than before," although the couple is still in bed and Friday is on the floor, this time with a scar around his neck. The narrator finds a yellowed leaf of paper and reads the words that begin this novel, that began Barton's description of her island sojourn: "At last I could row no further." The next phrase is Barton's, but it refers to the narrator's action: "With a sigh, making barely a splash, I slip overboard" (Coetzee, 155). But what have we, with the narrator, slipped overboard into? The narrator is now within the story, but not the story told by Barton, nor by Foe (nor by *Daniel Defoe, Author*). The narrator is presenting yet another version or vision, this time of the sunken slave ship, of the land beneath the ocean, dirty and filled with death. We are told that this is the same water "as yesterday, as last year, as three hundred years ago." When Friday is found, the narrator asks "what is this ship?" But this is a place beyond representation; it is a place we are told "where bodies are their own signs." Friday's mouth opens and we get the final paragraph of *Foe*, but we are not given answers, we do not have the novel wrapped up neatly for us, nor are we given an ending that suggests a pattern of closure. Instead, the last paragraph of *Foe* assigns more work to the reader, refuses to close, to stop:

> His mouth opens. From inside him comes a slow stream, without breath, without interruption. It flows up through his body and out upon me; it passes through the cabin, through the wreck; washing the cliffs and shores of the island, it runs northward and southward to the ends of the earth. Soft and cold, dark and unending, it beats against my eyelids, against the skin of my face. (Coetzee, 157)

The Text that is *Foe* and the many (gendered, racial, political, social) texts intersecting within it may *not* be fully deciphered, completed. Rather, *Foe* insists on active participation, on the attempted disentanglement of the threads that run through the novel. As Barthes explains in "The Death of the Author":

> In the multiplicity of writing, everything is to be *disentangled*, nothing *deciphered*; the structure can be followed, "run" (like the thread of a stocking) at every point and at every level, but there is nothing beneath: the space of writing is to be ranged over, not pierced. (1968, 147)

The structure that is 'run' takes the form of texts, and Barthes is surely correct in disallowing the reader the mistaken assurance of an absolute 'truth' underneath. But there is certainly *something* underneath the textual threads of *Foe*, just as there is something behind, above, beyond, and beside. Barthes's point is that all that can be 'beneath' would be the structure of more writing, more texts. This may be the case, but we also need to remember that these 'texts' are made up of lives. And this is part of *Foe's* text. The final image of *Foe* helps us to visualize the structure of texts: a stream, unending waves washing against us, running to the ends of the earth. Ultimately, *Foe's* text refuses to 'represent' Friday's story, it refuses readability. It ends without ending, remaining and dictating process and refusing its status as product. Lest, however, I get too caught up in my presentation of *Foe* as Text, I need to remember Barthes's admonishment that it would be futile to try to materially separate works from Texts. I did, after all pay $15.95 for my copy of *Foe*, it is found on book lists and library shelves, and is currently being used as a teaching tool.

When Barthes next discusses the Text as that which can be experienced "in reaction to the sign" (1971, 158), we are reminded once again of the representational closure expected by the sign consisting of an unproblematic signified and signifier. Barthes states:

> The work closes on a signified. There are two modes of signification which can be attributed to this signified: either it is claimed to be evident and the work is then the object of a literal science . . . or else it is considered to be secret, ultimate, something to be sought out . . . ; in short, the work itself functions as a general sign. . . . The Text, on the contrary, practices the infinite deferment of the signified, is dilatory; its field is that of the signifier and the signifier must not be conceived of as "the first stage of meaning," its material vestibule, but, in complete opposition to this, as its *deferred action*. (1971, 158)

Barthes's point is one we are familiar with: the infinity of the signifier refers not to some ultimate ineffable idea, but rather, refuses closure, and refers to a 'play'.

Barthes's distinction between work and Text here is couched in the same language that is often used to distinguish traditional (to modern) fiction from postmodern fiction, and for the most part I think these parallel distinctions hold up. But as I hope to have made clear by now, no description can be exact, and it is precisely the nature of postmodern fiction, as it is of the Text, to defy limits and to refuse description. More to the point, there are novels which operate within a postmodern moment and foreground their own textuality, but may still be recuperated by (or read as) the closed structure known as the work. Similarly, there are novels which have been read for years as works, which, because of a shift in reading strategies or paradigms, open up as Texts (see Spanos, 1987, 206–07).

Michel Tournier's *Friday* is one example of a novel which, despite its many postmodern moments, and its obvious rich intertextuality, may ultimately be recuperated into the logic of the work. Whereas the Text is "like language, . . . structured but off-centered, without closure" (Barthes, 1971, 159), *Friday*'s structure is quite specifically guided by the urge for closure. We may say that this novel is structured much like a moment *within* it: Crusoe, in the process of covering his island with remembered aphorisms from *Poor Richard's Almanack*, considers painting 'He who kills a sow destroys her progeny unto the thousandth generation; he who squanders a crown piece destroys a mountain of sovereigns' "on 114 goats, one letter to each goat, and let[ting] chance determine when, in the course of their endless permutations, they would arrange themselves in the right order and reveal the message" (Tournier, 132). This is a genuinely postmodern impulse, as are many of the impulses of the novel. But Crusoe does *not* carry out this idea. Similarly, although *Friday* contains texts which are congruent with the postmodern moment, such as the enactment of the relationship between power and subjectivity discussed in the previous chapter, its symbolic structure is finally, I believe, closed off. This takes place in at least two ways. First, there is the Tarot reading in the Prologue which serves to enclose the text of *Friday* within myth. And second, there is the circular, if spiraling, structure of the story itself: when Friday 'escapes' he is replaced by the white boy, Jaan (named "Sunday" by Crusoe), who becomes the new son to join Crusoe in a new life. Thus, in the end of this novel is Crusoe's rebirth, or beginning. In the terms we have discussed thus far, *Friday* may contain 'texts'—in fact, I will suggest later that it would be impossible for it not to—but it comes to rest as a work. *Foe*, on the other hand, bears the markings of the work, but its play and its insistence on the reader's involvement place it in the realm of the text.

The Text, says Barthes, "is plural." This is not another way of saying that it allows for a number of varied interpretations, but rather, that it is "an *irreducible* (and not merely acceptable) plural" (1971, 159). And this irreducible plurality is directly related to the text's intertextuality. The text is "woven entirely with citations, references, echoes, cultural languages . . . antecedent or contemporary, which cut across it through and through in a vast stereophony" (1971, 160). Julia Kristeva states it this way: "any text is constructed as a mosaic of quotations; any text is the absorption and transformation of another" (1986, 37). Both Kristeva and Barthes caution, however, that this mosaic, the 'intertextual' in which every text is held, is not to be confused with some origin of the text:

> to try to find the "sources," the "influences" of a work,
> is to fall in with the myth of filiation; the citations which
> go to make up a text are anonymous, untraceable, and
> yet *already read*: they are quotations without inverted
> commas. (Barthes, 1971, 160)

The distinction between intertextuality and source studies is crucial and too often ignored. It is the work that is "caught up in a process of filiation," that provides the place for homage to representations of the father—be it author or previous work. In short, the work and its filial position belong to a logic of origins, a logic post-structuralists refuse in reference to the chain of signifiers *without* signified. The work, as mentioned, belongs to a logic *of* the signified.

This is not to say, of course, that a study of intertextuality has nothing to do with what has come 'before'. Intertextuality is precisely a momentary compendium of everything that has come before and is now. Intertextuality calls attention to prior texts in the sense that it acknowledges that no text can have meaning without those prior texts, it is a space where 'meanings' intersect. There is no such creature as the autonomous text (or work). Jonathan Culler explains it thus:

> "intertextuality" leads us to consider prior texts as con-
> tributors to a code which makes possible the various

effects of signification. Intertextuality thus becomes less a name for a work's relation to particular prior texts than a designation of its participation in the discursive space of a culture: the relationship between a text and the various languages or signifying practices of a culture and its relation to those texts which articulate for it the possibilities of that culture. (1981, 103)

This is to say that the intertextuality of *Foe*, for example, may have very little to do with that 1719 work *Robinson Crusoe*, but has very much to do with the political text whose thread 'runs' well beyond the silencing of the black voice (the tongueless Friday) in Coetzee's native South Africa through the entire history of colonialization. It has very much to do with the textual thread unraveling through the absent histories of women, or through histories not told from the woman's point of view because within particular historical and cultural frameworks women are invisible. We remember Barton's query to herself as she begins to write "The Female Castaway. Being a True Account of a Year Spent on a Desert Island. With Many Strange Circumstances Never Hitherto Related":

> Dubiously I thought: Are these enough strange circumstances to make a story of? How long before I am driven to invent new and stranger circumstances: the salvage of tools and muskets from Cruso's ship; the building of a boat, or at least a skiff . . . a landing by cannibals on the island, followed by a skirmish and many bloody deaths. (Coetzee, 67)

Coetzee's novel gives one possible answer to her question, reminding us of the circumstances presented in the novel *Robinson Crusoe* ("who lived eight and twenty years, all alone . . ."). These are just two of the textual threads that run through *Foe*. There is also, of course, the postmodern literary narratological text which problematizes the notion of history as representable through the by-now-familiar technique of postmodern historical parody, which Linda

Hutcheon refers to as "repetition with critical difference" (1985, 6)—
a definition not without its own reference to intertextuality. (A related
postmodern strategy is the development of what Hutcheon calls 'historiographic metafiction'—see Chapter 5.) Intertextuality is not simply a reference to earlier texts, but is a manipulation of those texts
as well. In Kristeva's words: "a text works by absorbing and destroy-
ing at the same time the other texts of the intertextual space" (Kristeva, 1969, 257).

That the strategy of 'obvious' intertextuality may be read within
a postmodern paradigm is made clear by Hutcheon in *A Poetics of
Postmodernism*:

> among the many things that postmodern intertextuality
> challenges are both closure and single, centralized mean-
> ing. Its willed and willful provisionality rests largely
> upon its acceptance of the inevitable textual infiltration
> of prior discursive practices. (1988, 127)

More specifically, the strategy of *Foe* may be read as part of an

> [i]ntertextual parody of canonical American and Euro-
> pean classics [which] is one mode of appropriating and
> reformulating—with significant change—the dominant
> white, male, middle-class, heterosexual, Eurocentric cul-
> ture. It does not reject it, for it cannot. Postmodernism
> signals its dependence by its *use* of the canon, but reveals
> its rebellion through its ironic *abuse* of it. (Hutcheon,
> 1988, 130)

Kristeva's use of the term intertextuality refers to an arena much
larger than the example I have been using here of postmodern fiction.
Her realm is that of semiotics, and thus intertextuality is seen in the
context of the passage from one sign-system to another:

> this process comes about through a combination of dis-
> placement and condensation. . . . It also involves an al-

tering of the thetic *position*—the destruction of the old
position and the formation of a new one. The new signifying system may be produced with the same signifying material; in language, for example, the passage may
be made from narrative to text, or it may be borrowed
from different signifying materials; the transposition
from a carnival scene to the written text, for instance.
In this connection we examined the formation of a specific signifying system—the novel—as the result of a re-
distribution of several different sign-systems: carnival,
courtly poetry, scholastic discourse. The term *intertextuality* denotes this transposition of one (or several) sign-
system(s) into another. (Kristeva, 1986a, 111)

Kristeva's words here remind us of Derrida's "supplement"—a
replacement that is always excessive. Derrida indicates the symbiotic
relationship of "supplement" and "writing," and, I would add, intertextuality, when he says: "there has never been anything but writing; there has never been anything but supplements, substitutive significations which could only come forth in a chain of differential
references" (1976, 172–73). A chain of differential references is yet
another way of describing the inter-texts of a text.

One result of emphasizing intertextuality, that is, the irreducible
plurality of texts that are part of any one particular text, is, as mentioned at the beginning of this chapter, a refocusing of critical attention from the position of the subject (the author) to the notion
of textual productivity. If we see the locus of textual meaning as
taking place within the history of discourse itself, then a literary
work can no longer be considered original; "if it were, it could have
no meaning for its reader. It is only as part of a prior discourse that
any text derives meaning and significance" (Hutcheon, 1988, 126).
Barthes discusses this refocusing as a refusal of the myth of filiation,
in which

[t]he author is reputed the father and the owner of his
work: literary science therefore teaches *respect* for the

manuscript and the author's declared intentions. . . . As
for the Text, it reads without the inscription of the Father.
(1971, 160–61)

Barthes uses the metaphor of the organism in association with the
work: something that grows and develops—it has a linear logic, a
beginning and an ending. The metaphor of the Text, however, is that
of the network: "if the Text extends itself, it is as a result of a
combinatory systematic" (1971, 161). The Text is thus owed no vital
"respect" as it may be read "without the guarantee of its father, the
restitution of the inter-text paradoxically abolishing any legacy"
(1971, 161).

Barthes's metaphoric distinction between a logic of the organism
and of the network, in which the Text is a particular moment in
which the cross-hatching of "a combinatory systematic" is momentarily evident, goes a long way toward separating the work from the
text. But it still leaves some programmatic questions unanswered.
One question, which I have introduced, has to do with the presence
of 'texts' within a work. A second question has to do with how to
study the intertextuality of a text, when the very concept of intertextuality exists within a vastness that cannot be confined without
undoing the notion of intertextuality itself. As Kristeva states: "the
text is exactly that which cannot be thought within the whole conceptual system that grounds present-day understanding, for it is precisely that text which delineates the limits of that understanding"
(Kristeva, 1969a, 24). Perhaps a 'negative' example of this danger will
clarify my point. Harold Bloom's *Anxiety of Influence* (1973) suggests that poetic influence, when it involves "two strong, authentic
poets," takes place within an act of willful "misreading" of the prior
poet. In so doing the 'son' denies the 'father's' poetical paternity. As
such Bloom's theory partakes of the myth of filiation and joins the
realm of source studies. Culler points out:

> The function of Bloom's theory of influence, certainly
> the function of the Freudian analogies which structure
> it, is to keep everything in the family. . . . If Bloom's

"antithetical criticism" is ultimately a genetic theory
rather than a theory of the conditions of signification, it
nevertheless illustrates the dangers that beset the notion
of intertextuality: it is a difficult concept to use because
of the vast and undefined discursive space it designates,
but when one narrows it so as to make it more usable
one either falls into source study of a traditional and
positivistic kind (which is what the concept was designed
to transcend) or else ends by naming particular texts as
the pre-texts or grounds of interpretive convenience.
(1981, 108–09)

Culler's points are well taken, and his analysis of Bloom's theory
of origins, is, I believe, accurate. But his second criticism, of "naming
particular texts as the pre-texts or grounds of interpretive convenience," need not be seen as a literary evil. As readers, we can do much
worse than first to acknowledge the unknowability or uncontrollability of all the "anonymous, untraceable, and yet *already read*"
(Barthes, 1971, 160) citations that go to make up a text, and then
to proceed to acknowledge our own agendas as we 'read' Texts. A
brief example of this procedure is my discussion above of *Foe*, in
which I acknowledged that some of the texts I am interested in have
to do with gendered and racial silences, and how *Foe* 'absorbs and
destroys' those texts. In the process, *Foe's* author, Coetzee, must
disrupt the process of filiation within the text of *Foe*; he must displace
the notion of author/owner. Barthes explains that

> It is not that the Author may not "come back" in the
> Text, in his text, but he then does so as a "guest." If he
> is a novelist, he is inscribed in the novel like one of his
> characters, figured in the carpet; no longer privileged,
> paternal, aletheological, his inscription is ludic. . . . the
> *I* which writes the text, it too, is never more than a paper-
> *I*. (1971, 161)

This is one way we may read the entry of the narrator into *Foe*,
outside of narrative logic: to show not simply the caprice and the

uncontrollability of perspective, but more to the point, to act out the intertextuality of subjectivity itself. It makes the point that this particular text is both controlled and not controlled by an 'other', and that that 'other' is itself a text.

The narratological disruption in *Foe* also puts to work another subject—the reader. It had been possible, up until the last few pages of the novel, to sit back and to 'consume' the story. True, there had been questions left unanswered and mysteries unsettled (for example, who is the young woman who claims to be Barton's daughter?), but traditionally as readers we have been taught to read patiently, to wait, if not always for closure, then at least for the recognition of the pattern or structure through which to make sense of the novel. This is what Barthes means when he says that the work "is normally the object of a consumption" (1971, 161). The Text, however,

> (if only by its frequent "unreadability") decants the work (the work permitting) from its consumption and gathers it up as play, activity, production, practice. This means that the Text requires that one try to abolish (or at the very least to diminish) the distance between writing and reading, in no way by intensifying the projection of the reader into the work but by joining them in a single signifying practice. (1971, 162)

The "one" in the statement above can refer to the position of the writer as well as of the reader. In *Foe* that position is shared by the entry of the narrator of the last pages—the "one" who goes to work, not to "make" Friday speak, for example, nor to speak for him, but to listen to him, all the while recognizing his/her role in the production of *Foe* as a "signifying practice." This is what it means to continue to 'produce' the text, not to expect it to come to a close.

Barthes refers to this practice as "playing," a term we have become familiar with through Derrida's explanation of the play between signifer and signified (which then also becomes a signifier)—that moment, that space of possibility and meaning. Barthes explains that *reading*, in the sense of consuming, is far from *playing* with the text. "Playing" must be understood here in all its polysemy: the text itself *plays* (like a door, like a machine with "play") and the reader plays twice over, playing the Text as one plays a game, looking for a practice which re-produces it, but, in order that that practice not be reduced to a passive, inner *mimesis* (the Text is precisely that which resists such a reduction), also playing the Text in the musical sense of the term. (1971, 162)

Thus, the reader becomes a co-producer, a co-collaborator of the Text. The reader takes on shared responsibility for the text's 'meaning'. As a result the Text always remains in motion; it is process, not product. Barthes points out what readers of much postmodern fiction have come to experience:

The reduction of reading to a consumption is clearly responsible for the "boredom" experienced by many in the face of the modern ("unreadable") text, the avant-garde film or painting: to be bored means that one cannot produce the text, open it out, *set it going*. (1971, 163)

Thus, whereas the pleasure of the work is a pleasure of consumption ("unless by some exceptional critical effort" it becomes otherwise), the pleasure of the Text, as order of the signifier, is one of production.
    Barthes concludes his essay by saying that

the discourse on the Text should itself be nothing other than text, research, textual activity, since the Text is that *social* space which leaves no language safe, outside, nor any subject of the enunciation in position as judge, master, analyst, confessor, decoder. The theory of the Text can coincide only with a practice of writing. (1971, 164)

Earlier I suggested some criticisms of Barthes's distinction between work and text. First, there is just that—the absolute distinction—which presents a problem. Although Barthes's essay is invaluable in pointing out differences and in clarifying a shift in reading paradigms, his distinctions come to rest on the foundation of binarism, on an 'either/or' logic. My criticism follows the poststructuralist pattern of using and critiquing structuralist tenets, and then moving on. Barthes's distinctions have helped us to see how many contemporary Texts insist on the reader's participation in producing meaning. In the process, although Barthes speaks of the play of texts and of how there is nothing 'beneath' the writing, he effectively shifts the signifying position from writer/author to reader. The result is what must be a false sense of control. A poststructuralist response is to relinquish the control that was never ours, but not to relinquish responsibility; that is, to acknowledge that *both* work and Text must be read in terms of textuality and intertextuality, which cannot be closed down or contained. Derrida tells us that *"there is nothing outside of the text. . . .* there has never been anything but writing; there have never been anything but supplements" (1976, 158–59). There is nothing that is not a text. Thus, although the work may seek closure, may adhere to a logic of containment, it is still just as replete with text as are those Texts which Barthes describes. When Barthes replaces the place of privilege of writer with the reader he opens the process of 'producing' the text immensely, for the number of readers is, potentially, infinite. What we cannot forget, however, is that the reader also exists within textuality. How the reader 'plays' the score of the text will be determined by a combination of that reader's subject positions, depending on, for example, gender, race, education, age, geographical location, erotic identity and practice, position within family, ad infinitum. Each of these subject positions is itself a text. Frank Lentricchia in *After the New Criticism* makes this point, taking the Barthes's term of text a step further to speak of textuality (and thus, of intertextuality):

> The formalist's "text," or the traditional historicist's discourse of "literature," as fixed paddocks of meaning, yield to "textuality"—a potentially infinite and indefinite, all-inclusive series of networks of interrelation

whose connections and boundaries are not securable because they are ruled by never-ending movements of linguistic energy that recognize neither the rights of private
ownership nor the authority of structuralism's centralized government of interpretive norms. (1980, 189)

What this all comes down to, then, is not a refusal of Barthes's
definitions, but rather an insistence on the recognition that *everything* (Texts *and* works) is intertextual. In terms of our immediate
discussion, there is no limit to the texts within any one novel. For
example, we could begin by 'running' the 'thread' of the religious
text through *Friday*. We could follow innumerable strains here: the
historical practice of Bibliolotry and its cultural implications in total
reliance on the 'Word'; Crusoe replicating the patriarchy of God on
his island; the introduction of a Quaker sensibility and its relationship
to the Protestant/Calvinist work ethic; the relation between colo-
nialism and this work ethic; Crusoe's Christianity as myth and su-
perstition (think of his serendipitous choosing of Biblical passages
to reveal the truth, and more importantly of the relationship between
the reading of first the Bible and then the earth for signs); the relationship in Christianity between Father-worship and Sun/Son-wor-
ship. By running any one of the above threads we would come in
contact with a network of other texts: familial, historical, cultural,
social, mythical, etc.

And of course, *Friday*, like any Crusoe myth, is replete with
racial texts. It would be an interesting task, for example, to study
racial texts within the very limited scope of *Robinson Crusoe*, *Friday*,
and *Foe*, to analyze the implications of Friday as "Indian" (*Robinson
Crusoe*), as "half-caste" (*Friday*), as "Negro" (*Foe*). Or, we may well
ask, what texts are involved in Tournier's tale of a master/slave relationship that becomes the tale of brotherhood, but brotherhood
only as seen by the white man and told from the white man's point
of view?

Or, what are some of the sexual texts in *Friday* which cross with
the racial, the religious, and gendered texts? Crusoe says his relationship with Friday is not sexual, but then, has Crusoe been a reliable

judge of his emotions? When he discovers Friday's 'love-making' with
the island Speranza is his wrath solely due to the 'insult' to Speranza,
"outraged by a Negro" (Tournier, 167)? Or is it jealousy of another
type? Why is it so easy for Crusoe to quickly turn his anger toward
the inanimate earth, Speranza, as the adulterous woman? To attempt
this analysis is to find oneself within a web of a dozen intersecting
texts dealing with the perception of women (Biblically, historically,
culturally—particularly in the eighteenth century), as well as with
other colonializing texts of power and women. (We remember 'Speranza's' role as "female" in this novel: as that which is to be cultivated/
owned, to function as mother and wife, and then to be outgrown,
surpassed by the love of men for each other.) And if we are to read
Crusoe's relationship with Friday as asexual or brotherly, as Crusoe
protests, then why does the Tarot card which is meant to represent
this part of Crusoe's tale depict Friday as a Venus-character, as one
of a set of twins "attached by the neck to the feet of the bisexual
angel" (Tournier, 10)? There is certainly a distinction to be made
between bisexual and asexual. Crusoe says "that at no time has Friday
inspired me with any sodomite desire" (Tournier, 211) and yet he
has just described Friday thus:

> I watch Friday as he dives amid the breakers rolling up
> the beach; and the kind of dance in which he is engaged,
> the natural grace and elegance of his movements, the
> gaiety, the gleam of wet, firm flesh, all this brings to my
> mind the thought of Venus rising from the waves. (Tour-
> nier, 210)

These questions are not intended to make a case for Crusoe as ho-
mosexual, as much as to indicate the threads of other texts that we
could follow—for example, the eroticization of the master/slave relationship or the eroticization of the 'native' in colonialist literature.

Although these are just a few of the nexuses of a few texts in
Friday, my point is that no textual thread can 'run' out, for each
point along its path is also a node for a network of other texts. This
is one definition of intertextuality. Another definition could be put

in terms of the old saw that "there's nothing new under the sun." Every text is always already read. That is not to say that there is no such thing as shifts or change, but change usually has to do with perceiving a network of texts within some 'other' paradigm. For example, look at how the 'ideological' texts of the Robinson Crusoe myth shift through time in terms of Defoe's *Robinson Crusoe* and Tournier's *Friday*.

Since my project here has nothing to do with saying something 'new' about Defoe's book, I contain my remarks about its ideological/ economical text to a brief paraphrase of some of the points Ian Watt makes in his chapter on *"Robinson Crusoe*, individualism and the novel" in his 1957 book *The Rise of the Novel*. Watt's emphasis on individualism places us within a humanist ideology. Watt states that individualism depends on

> an economic and political organization which allows its members a very wide range of choices in their actions, and on an ideology primarily based on . . . the autonomy of the individual, irrespective of his particular social status or personal capacity. (60)

Watt identifies the 'causes' of the emergence of the 'individualist' in modern society as: "the rise of modern industrial capitalism and the spread of Protestantism, especially in its Calvinist or Puritan forms" (1957, 60). Within this frame of reference, then, Defoe's Robinson Crusoe is seen as a hero of "economic individualism": he methodically pursues money, works in reference to profit-and-loss bookkeeping, and enacts the Calvinist creed of the dignity of labor (as the untiring stewardship of the material gifts of God). Watt notes, however, that

> The basis for Robinson Crusoe's prosperity, of course, is the original stock of tools which he loots from the shipwreck; they comprise, we are told, "the biggest magazine of all kinds . . . that was ever laid up for one man." So Defoe's hero is not really a primitive nor a proletarian

> but a capitalist. . . . Crusoe is in fact the lucky heir to
> the labours of countless other individuals; his solitude is
> the measure, and the price of his luck, since it involves
> the fortunate decease of all the other potential stock-
> holders. (1957, 87–88)

Watt's own analysis thus debunks the ideology of capitalist individualism as based on an economic and political organization in
which each member can "make it on his own." Chapter 3 has discussed in some detail how this concept is based on a restricted mem-
bership: white, Christian, European, propertied men. With this understanding we recognize Barthes's point when he says that the work
cannot be re-written—"it is impossible today to write 'like that' "
(1971, 163).

Although Tournier's Crusoe looks over his shoulder at Defoe's
character, today, only a parody of *Robinson Crusoe* is possible. The
ideological/economics text in *Friday* looks to other texts. A com-
panion piece for *Friday* is less likely to be a volume which recounts
the development of capitalism, than, for example, the Marxist Louis
Althusser's essay "Ideology and Ideological State Apparatuses." I am
not suggesting that in writing *Friday*, Tournier set out to write a
Marxist text, or to rewrite *Robinson Crusoe* from a Marxist perspective—there would be no way to prove that, and Tournier's intentions are not really important here anyway. Rather, in this discussion of intertextuality my purpose is to show how a Marxist text,
and thus, a continuing of ideological/economic texts, may be read
within a particular fictional work. My point is that the evolution of
Tournier's Robinson Crusoe from capitalist to egalitarian need not
be read as an ideological change in heart brought on by an increasing
drive toward the brotherhood of man, but rather, as the result of his
inability to inculcate Friday into his own ideological frame of reference, and thus, his inability to fulfill the ultimate condition of
production, that is: "the reproduction of the conditions of production" (Althusser, 1971, 127). Althusser's point in this particular essay
is that Ideological State Apparatuses (ISAs) reproduce their own con-

ditions of production. My point is that Crusoe fails to inculcate Friday into his Ideological State Apparatuses.

Althusser explains:

> the reproduction of labour power requires . . . a repro-
> duction of its submission to the rules of the established
> order, i.e. a reproduction of submission to the ruling
> ideology for the workers, and a reproduction of the abil-
> ity to manipulate the ruling ideology correctly for the
> agents of exploitation and repression. . . . In other words,
> the school (but also other State institutions like the
> Church, or other apparatuses like the Army) teaches
> "know-how," but in forms which ensure *subjection to
> the ruling ideology* or the mastery of its "practice."
> (1971, 132)

The jump to *Friday* is easy when we think of how Crusoe specifically sees himself in the "roles of Governor, Commander in Chief,
and Spiritual Pastor" (Tournier, 144). In order to fulfill these roles
completely, however, Crusoe needs Friday, otherwise he has only himself to govern, command, and minister to. Not that he doesn't do
all three for himself before Friday arrives. Crusoe's 'civilization', complete with charter, penal code, fortress, and meeting house, is in place
well before Friday arrives at his feet. Crusoe is able to mimic the
society he knows of Great Britain for himself, but he needs an 'other'
to reproduce Crusoe's island civilization. And although this reproduction must ultimately be terminal—he cannot reconstitute "labour
power" through an increasing population—Crusoe can, through Friday, see his civilization mirrored back to him, and thus, re-produced.
But this does not happen automatically; Crusoe, as the State, must
inculcate Friday into the State's ideology, that is, into a way of thinking that is assumed to be 'natural'.

Althusser talks of Marx's conception of the structure of society
as constituted by economic base and the superstructure, which itself
contains two 'levels': the politico-legal (law and the State) and ideology (the different ideologies, religious, ethical, legal, political, etc.)

(1971, 134). Althusser states that it is "possible and necessary to think what characterizes the essential of the existence and nature of the superstructure *on the basis of reproduction*" (1971, 136). In the Marxist tradition, explains Althusser, the State is explicitly conceived as a repressive apparatus. The State equals the State apparatuses which equals police, courts, prison, plus the army, head of state, government, administration. Althusser makes his addition by noting that

> to advance the theory of the State it is indispensable to take into account not only the distinction between *State power* and *State apparatus*, but also another reality which is clearly on the side of the (repressive) State apparatus, but must not be confused with it. I shall call this reality by its concept: *the ideological State apparatuses*. (1971, 142)

The Ideological State Apparatuses (ISAs) are not to be confused with the (repressive) State apparatus; rather, they are "realities which present themselves to the immediate observer in the form of distinct and specialized institutions": the religious ISA (the system of different churches), the educational ISA (the system of the different public and private 'Schools'), the family ISA, the legal ISA, the political ISA (the political system, including the different Parties), the trade-union ISA, the communications ISA (press, radio and television, etc.), the cultural ISA (Literature, the Arts, sports, etc.) (1971, 143).

Althusser's distinction between the (repressive) State Apparatus and the ISAs is clear:

> the (Repressive) State Apparatus functions massively and predominantly *by repression* (including physical repression), while functioning secondarily by ideology. . . . Ideological State Apparatuses function massively and predominantly *by ideology*, but they also function secondarily by repression. (1971, 145)

Most importantly, despite the diversity and contradictions of the ISAs, they function according to a unified ideology which is that of *the ruling ideology*, which is the ideology of "the ruling class." Given the fact that the "ruling class" in principle holds State power ... and therefore has at its disposal the (Repressive) State Apparatus, we can accept the fact that this same ruling class is active in the Ideological State Apparatuses insofar as it is ultimately the ruling ideology which is realized in the Ideological State Apparatuses, precisely in its contradictions. ... To my knowledge, *no class can hold State power over a long period without at the same time exercising its hegemony over and in the State Ideological Apparatuses.* (1971, 146)

Within the framework of *Friday*, Crusoe's (repressive) State apparatus is successful. He assures Friday's obedience as long as he is 'master': "All that [Friday's] master ordered was right, all that he forbade was wrong. It was good to toil night and day for the functioning of an elaborate system that served no purpose" (Tournier, 140). But this is obviously a very different situation from affecting the 'ideology' of Friday, which must be done through Ideological State Apparatuses if Crusoe is to hold his (State) power over a long period. And it is clear that Crusoe's ISAs are not recognized by Friday. Think for example of the religious ISA of the island, and of Friday's unfortunate reaction to Crusoe's insistence that he repeat religious and moral axioms which Crusoe propounded:

> For example—"God is an all-powerful, omniscient master, infinitely good, merciful and just, the Creator of Man and of All Things." And Friday's laugh rang out, irrepressible, lyrical, and blasphemous, to be extinguished like a snuffed candle by a resounding blow on the cheek. This image of a merciful, all-powerful God had seemed to him irresistibly comic in the light of his own brief experience of life. But no matter; in a voice now trembling with sobs he dutifully repeated his master's words. (Tournier, 140–41)

There is little doubt but that Crusoe's own shortsightedness must be blamed for Friday's remaining outside, and thus, unable to reproduce (in the sense of mirroring), the ideology of Crusoe and his island State. Quite simply, Crusoe chooses to dominate through repression rather than ideology. As a result Friday remains separate, other—he does not become 'like' Crusoe, he does not come to see Crusoe's civilization as natural. Crusoe does not make his ideological superstructure meaningful in any way to Friday.

We may further clarify why Friday does not come to recognize Crusoe's ideology as his own by looking at the connection Althusser makes between ideology and subjectivity. Althusser defines ideology through two theses: "Ideology represents the imaginary relationship of individuals to their real conditions of existence" (1971, 162), and "Ideology has a material existence" (1971, 165). He explains:

> where only a single subject (such and such an individual) is concerned, the existence of the ideas of his belief is material in that *his ideas are his material actions inserted into material practices governed by material rituals which are themselves defined by the material ideological apparatus from which derive the ideas of that subject.* (1971, 169)

This is precisely where the connection between subjectivity and ideology becomes evident. Althusser states that ideology 'interpellates' individuals as subjects: that is, hails or calls, in such a way that the 'hailed to' recognizes her/himself as the object of that 'hail'.

We need to read 'interpellation' with a mind to the poststructuralist critiques of representation and subjectivity that we discussed in earlier chapters:

> Like all obviousnesses, including those that make a word "name a thing" or "have a meaning" (therefore including the obviousness or the "transparency" of language), the "obviousness" that you and I are subjects—and that that does not cause any problems—is an ideological effect, the

elementary ideological effect. It is indeed a peculiarity of ideology that it imposes (without appearing to do so, since these are "obviousnesses") obviousnesses as obviousnesses, which we cannot *fail to recognize* and before which we have the inevitable and natural reaction of crying out (aloud or in the "still, small voice of conscience"): "That's obvious! That's right! That's true!" (1971, 172)

And this is, of course, the point which Friday never comes close to in terms of Crusoe's world. Far from being obvious, right, or true, Crusoe's world to Friday is alternately the cause for confusion and amusement—that is, until that particular world crumbles, literally. In short, Crusoe's ISAs fail to 'recruit' or 'interpellate' Friday as a subject of Crusoe's State. In Althusser's words:

> ideology has always-already interpellated individuals as subjects, which amounts to making it clear that individuals are always-already interpellated by ideology as subjects, which necessarily leads us to one last proposition: *individuals are always-already subjects.* . . . Before its birth, the child is . . . always-already a subject, appointed as a subject in and by the specific familial ideological configuration in which it is 'expected'. . . . [I]t is in this implacable and more or less 'pathological' . . . structure that the former subject-to-be will have to 'find' 'its' place, i.e. 'become' the sexual subject (boy or girl) which it already is in advance. (1971, 176)

But this is *not* the case for Friday in Crusoe's world. Friday was, of course, born into a subjectivity, but not one recognizable within Crusoe's world, which Friday enters as if through a time machine.

Crusoe, of course, immediately recognizes the opportunity for, and takes on, the subject position of master/owner. And Friday has no alternative but to docilely recognize his new subject position as slave. As slave, Friday's behavior is consistent within a master/slave ideology. It is the interpellation of Friday as subject to Crusoe's ISAs that remains unsuccessful, and thus, once the master/Crusoe is out of the picture, if only temporarily (that is, at the moment Friday notices the island master/slave ritual suspended, with the suspension of the water clock), then Friday owes nothing to Crusoe's civilization. He is immediately outside of Crusoe's jurisdiction. Crusoe's ISAs (centered around the church) have been weak; only as a (Repressive) State Apparatus has Crusoe controlled Friday. Crusoe's ISAs did not lead Friday to think of Crusoe's very being and way of life as 'obvious', 'right', or 'true', and thus, Friday is not interpellated as a subject within Crusoe's 'ruling' ideology. Because Crusoe's Ideological State Apparatuses fail, Friday does not 'work' by himself. When Crusoe leaves, Friday turns his island upside down: he remains antithetical to the cultivated island.

The above is, of course, just one fragment of a possible text within the novel *Friday*. The threads that we could follow within this novel, as within any novel are limitless. And this is precisely my point: despite the structure of *Friday* as a 'work' and not a 'Text', it must nonetheless be made up of texts, it must be itself 'textuality'. Once again, only by being intertextual, that is, already read, can something have meaning, otherwise it would exist in a vacuum. The word 'meaning', however, can be problematical. As I just used it, 'meaning' has to do with being recognizable, being capable of being read. Much postmodern fiction, however, is not afraid to also equate 'meaning' with 'purpose'. Although it rejects all-encompassing, absolute, and timeless truths, this fiction often deals with the marginalized or untold texts. Such fiction is often presented in the form of parody. The fictional device of historical parody with a purpose, known as historiographical metafiction, provides the background for Chapter 5.

5

Counter-Memory and Historiographic Metafiction:

Christa Wolf's *Cassandra*,
Timothy Findley's *Famous Last Words*,
Salman Rushdie's *Midnight's Children*

The concerns of the postmodern moment discussed thus far are reflected in contemporary re-evaluations of the concept of history, both in historiography and in literature. For example, the critique of representation translates into a refusal to see the past as constituted by events which we can innocently recapture and re-present through language. We no longer are able to think about absolute and unquestionable 'facts' or 'truths' of history, speaking now of 'histories' instead of History. Our emphasis now on signification, rather than validation, we ask: how have we, or do we, give meaning to events through interpretation? In the realm of historiography (the telling of history in narrative form) we see suggested answers to these questions in concepts such as Hayden White's (1973) concept of 'metahistory', which posits historiography as a poetic construct. That is, the historian works within a 'metahistorical' paradigm which exists on a poetic, or linguistic, level, and which determines what, for that historian, constitutes historical explanations.

This emphasis on signification points to an increased awareness of the role of the interpreter, and thus, to questions of subjectivity, as well as to the intertextual nexus within which interpretation takes place. History, within the postmodern moment, must be 'read', first, through the act of enunciation in which historical 'texts' are produced, and second, within a particular historical, social, and political context. The poststructuralist decentering of the subject from the position from which reason emanates means that we may no longer perceive of history as a linear construct which places the subject, in the present, in the privileged position of making sense of all that has come before—as if the subject were either 'outside' of history, or else the final moment toward which all history has marched. Derrida pointed out that we are never 'outside' the labyrinth of discourse, we are never outside of a point of view or perspective which is always situated as a systemic function, within textuality.

One criticism of this concept of everything-as-'textuality' has been that it may be seen as an "infinite and indefinite, all-inclusive series of networks of interrelation whose connections and boundaries are not securable because they are ruled by never-ending movements of linguistic energy" (Lentricchia, 1980, 189), and thus may function as a transcendental of sorts. This is where Michel Foucault's methodology, with its emphasis on temporal and spatial contexts, becomes crucial. Foucault's methodology is consistent with the Derridean project of decentering, *différance*, and free play as he, too, rejects a representational/mimetic reconstruction of history. Foucault, however, reins in the Derridean project through his emphasis on textuality as contextualized by a set of rules that is always subject to historical transformation (Lentricchia, 1980, 189). Foucault emphasizes the aspect of power in terms of how 'writing', in the sense of that which signifies, changes temporally and culturally. And since his emphasis on power leads to questions concerning which discourses have been 'historically' privileged (that is, which histories get told, and by whom?), we return to the postmodern critique of subjectivity to see that traditionally, the discourse of Western history has been presented within the discourse of the subject as white and male. Contemporary histories not only deal with the decentering of the present subject from the position of knowledge and meaning, but also with the interrogation of the past from ex-centric positions (for example, from the subject positions of women, gays, people of color, Jews, and so forth) (see Hutcheon, 1988, 57–73).

To return to an earlier statement: the 'act of enunciation' through which historical texts are produced refers to the subject positions of the producer and the receiver of texts. The postmodern project is dedicated to privileging neither the producer or the receiver within that situation, *nor* the text itself. In fact, one postmodern tenet is that the 'text' (be it literary or historical) may not be apprehended as separate from the producer or receiver. Rather, we look at how the text is given meaning within the entire enunciative act. In the Foucauldian terms which we will be using in this chapter, the project is to look at the will to power—evidenced through the will to knowledge, or interpretation—at work among the interactive subject positions. Who tells history? In whose name? To what purpose? The related postmodern project in reference to history is to identify the historical, social, and cultural contexts within which the enunciative act takes place. In Foucauldian terms, this becomes the temporal and spatial "discursive formation" within which meaning is produced.

For Foucault, history is not something that can be mastered or understood; rather, it consists of a web, a matrix, a network of intertexts or discourses. The Foucault I discuss in this chapter (his ideas and strategies were consistently reworked) is the Foucault of "Nietzsche, Genealogy, History" (1977), with reference to the Foucault of *The Archaeology of Knowledge* (1972). For Foucault's historian-as-genealogist, the particular and the local become the foci, not the universal and the transcendental. His attempt is to study a particular node within the intertextual network of a particular history—not to make the past make sense in terms of the present, but rather, to attempt to look at events in the past from the perspective of that particular past, that is, within its own particular discursive formation. This discursive formation consists of, binds together, and is reinforced by a complex group of relations "established between institutions, economic and social processes, behavioral patterns, systems of norms, techniques, types of classification, modes of characterization" (Foucault, 1972, 45). To speak of a discursive formation is to speak of the logic of a specific place and time (in the sense of ideology, 'commonsense' assumptions about the way things are). This discursive formation goes beyond the rationality of a place and time; it is, rather, what enables that rationality to appear as rational.

To be outside of a culture's discursive formation, then, is to be meaningless, or mad, or sick, or in some way on the margins. Foucault's histories often show how the meaning of the 'object' changes through time with the changing discursive formations. The Foucauldian project places the onus on the historian to resist making sense of the past through the present, while interrogating the sense-making *of* the past or *of* the 'other'. There is no assumption at work within the postmodern project about there being no such thing as a 'real' past; there is, rather, a recognition that the past is only available to us through various (and often contradictory) texts or discourses.

A baffling but consistent criticism about postmodernism—which usually gives to the postmodern an ontological status, instead of speaking of specific postmodern projects—is that it is ahistorical.[1] In fact, a historical sense is integral to the postmodern project. Granted, postmodernist fiction rejects any totalizing view of history, as does Foucault, choosing instead to problematize the very notion of historical knowledge. At the same time, postmodernist fiction problematizes the claim of art as the medium of transcendental, universal values. Foucault insists on contextualizing the notion of textuality; postmodern fiction enacts within its text "the context-dependent nature of all values." Foucault's genealogy highlights discontinuities and fractures; postmodern fiction challenges "narrative singularity and unity in the name of multiplicity and disparity" (Hutcheon, 1988, 90). The postmodern awareness is that *both* history and literature are discourses, and thus not to be talked of in terms of truth, as much as 'whose truth'. History then, in Foucault's terms, may become 'counter-memory': the process of reading history against its grain, of taking an acknowledged active role in the interpretation of history rather than a passive, viewing role. Counter-memory *intervenes* in history rather than *chronicles* it. This intervention is precisely the role of the postmodern literature which Linda Hutcheon has called 'historiographic metafiction'. The historiographic metafictionist refuses the possibility of looking to and writing about the past "as it really was." Rather s/he takes on an active role, and 'does' the past, participates, questions, and interrogates. In short, the project of the historiographic metafictionist is the Foucauldian project of counter-memory: and they are both historical and political. Throughout this chapter, I look more closely at counter-memory through Foucault's essay "Nietzsche, Genealogy, History" and three historiographic metafictions: Christa Wolf's *Cassandra*, Timothy Findley's *Famous Last Words*, and Salman Rushdie's *Midnight's Children*.

I stated earlier that postmodernism highlights the enunciative act in which all texts (all texts being historical) are produced. In an earlier chapter I spoke of the enunciating positions (the producer and the receiver of the text) as subject positions. Historiographic *metafiction* highlights the interaction and relationships of these subject positions as they work to give 'meaning' to the text; often the relationship between the position of the producer and of the receiver is actually inscribed, or placed, within the text itself. The position of the postmodern author is, as Hutcheon (1983) points out, still one of discursive authority. The author-function, which, of course, operates within larger cultural discourses, produces a text which manipulates (overtly or covertly) a reader-receiver. In the metafiction of postmodernism, this producing position is often given form through the narrator-author inscribed within the text, who openly acknowledges to the reader his or her presence and his or her power of manipulation. The result is often an insistence that the reader be aware of her/his complicity in determining any 'meaning' from the text. This is not to say that the narrator-author and reader work together to discover a meaning that is *within* the text; rather, the postmodern metafictionist challenges the reader to recognize that together they *determine* meaning. Such challenges and possibilities are evident in Timothy Findley's *Famous Last Words*, which manipulates the reader by conflating historical 'fact' and 'fiction', thus insisting that the reader accept his/her position not only as receiver, but also as joint producer in the telling and retelling of history. Contrary to the humanist paradigm, in which the enunciating entity (the producer) is suppressed (in the name of realism, empiricism, objectivity), within the postmodernist paradigm, the producer *and* the receiver are "situated" within "the enunciative act itself, and . . . within the broader historical, social, and political (as well as intertextual) context implied by that act" (Hutcheon, 1988, 75). The question "who is speaking?" is a consistent postmodern refrain, often meaning, "from what positions of power or authority, as producers (or interpreters) of texts, do we speak?"

In *Famous Last Words* the postmodernist author-function Findley usurps the modernist Pound's Romantic creation, Hugh Selwyn Mauberley, to tell a story which Mauberley defines as history but acknowledges to be much fiction. The power wielded by the narrator-author within the text (represented by Mauberley) is concurrently thrust upon and shared by the inscribed readers (represented by Lieutenant Quinn and Captain Freyberg) who together must determine the meaning of the text. Mauberley is still "out of key with his time," and thus is surprised to find himself playing the role of messenger within an international cabal—involving Charles Lindberg, Edward VIII and Wallis Warfield Simpson, and an assortment of top Nazi officials, British statesmen, and international businessmen and financiers—which actively manipulates the events of the time, those of World War II. Within the sphere of the novel, Mauberley becomes a historian, a messenger through time, who scratches a 'lost' version of history on the walls of two suites in an Austrian hotel in 1945. Mauberley recalls the events of this cabal while he waits to be murdered, precisely because he has this history to tell and the means with which to tell it. When an American troop finds the dead Mauberley, Lt. Quinn and Capt. Freyberg become the readers of the 'writing on the wall'. Lt. Quinn hopes that the text will expiate Mauberley; Capt. Freyberg expects it to damn him.

In short, *Famous Last Words* places us in the postmodernist position, once removed: we not only watch the position of the enunciating entity, the narrator-author (Mauberley) write, but we also see our own position as reader represented by Quinn and Freyberg. In the process, we are asked to think less about the modernist view of history as something which may be known, albeit from various perspectives, than of the postmodernist view of history as discourse, as something that is manipulated first by the teller, and then by the receiver. Just as importantly, we think about which histories are told within certain temporal and spatial contexts, as well as the factor of chance involved. We think of the histories not written or written only to disappear (as the walls of the hotel are to disappear at the end of the novel, to be defaced or blown up). The question historiographic metafiction raises, then, is not what is the 'true' history, but rather, *who* presents *what* history, and *who* reads and interprets it, toward *what* purpose? We not only watch the postmodern narrator-author write; we are also made aware that the writer is writing quite consciously for us. The narrator-author challenges the reader to participate in creating the picture. And the reader must comply, if only in the attempt to make sense of the text.

So much for who presents and who receives, but what about the *what* that is presented? As we watch Mauberley writing on the walls, his subjects are the focal point of the cabal, the Duke and Duchess of Windsor, or more accurately, the former King Edward VIII and Wallis Warfield Simpson, the woman who would be queen. But we see the subjects of Mauberley's work only in the background, as if through a glass, darkly; that is, we see the hazy outlines of two individuals who have made it into history textbooks. *Famous Last Words* suggests that our understanding of these figures pales in comparison to a hidden story such as Mauberley could give us. But reading the story on Mauberley's walls is only a transitory accident: only by chance do we hear of the Windsors' involvement in a cabal that contains names such as Hess, von Ribbontrop, and Lindberg. *Famous Last Words* suggests just one of an infinite set of possibilities or stories that will never be known.

The point is *not* that here is a possible 'true' revelation. Quite explicitly, the doubly fictional Mauberley begins his engraved walls with: "All I have written here is true; except the lies" (Findley, 59). Still, *Famous Last Words* moves beyond the truism that history is story, that any telling requires the perspective of a teller, and thus, the capricious or manipulative selection of detail. *Famous Last Words* is also a discussion of the elements of power and chance contained in any discourse, reminding us that the concepts of history and fiction can never be severed because both are discourse, and discourse constitutes and is constituted by a web of power relations. As Hutcheon (1983) states:

> discourse constitutes more than a repository of meaning; it involves both the potential for manipulation—through rhetoric or through the power of language and the vision that it creates—and also the possibility (if not permissibility) of evasion of responsibility through silence. (41)

We are asked to think about the power of discourse from the direction of the story that gets told: if the writings on the wall alter our perception of history, and thus, of reality, then the writer has taken on great authority. On the other hand, it is the nature of postmodern discourse, as seen in *Famous Last Words*, to simultaneously assign responsibility to the reader. A paradox emerges: the writer takes control and manipulates the reader into the position of taking on responsibility.

From another perspective, however, chance becomes the element of power. Chance allows Mauberley's walls to be read before they are defaced; chance prevents them from being further made known. Mauberley notes the arbitrariness of how chance and bias determine what is to be remembered:

> So this is history as she is never writ, I thought. Some day far in the future, some dread academic, much too careful of his research, looking back through the biased glasses of a dozen other "historians," will set this moment down on paper. And will get it wrong. Because he will not acknowledge that history is made in the electric moment, and its flowering is all in chance. (Findley, 180)

But the chance stories that unexpectedly come the reader's way may not alter the 'truths' the reader 'knows' anyway. Quinn reads the walls, wanting to believe that Mauberley (the Pro-Fascist) is ultimately without guilt, and after reading, says that the walls prove nothing. Freyberg, who expects to find justification for his career in vengeance, does. They read the same walls; their views are unchanged. Neither has learned the modernist lesson—that truth may be a matter of perspective; certainly, neither is ready for the postmodernist lesson—that the question is really one of available truths or stories, and the suppression of untold stories. Although it is chance that makes Mauberley's variation of history available to the readers Quinn and Freyberg, the interpretation of that history is then contested between the viewpoints, the ideologies, of these readers. *Famous Last Words* also presents readers for Mauberley's walls other than Quinn and Freyberg; he also 'presents' us. And our capacity for recognizing other perspectives is tested as we attempt to take control. Thus, an analysis of *Famous Last Words* reveals a network of relationships among Mauberley and the subjects of his text, the readers Quinn and Freyberg, the enunciating position of author-function held by Findley, and finally, the receivers, us.

We need to go beyond analyzing how this network of relationships participates in the production of the text, to the potential for increased awareness in historiographic metafiction. In presenting obviously manipulated versions, historiographic metafictionists call attention to the manipulation and caprice behind any story presented as 'truth'. The

> overt, self-conscious control by an inscribed narrator-author figure . . . demands, by its manipulation, the imposition of a single perspective, while *at the same time* subverting all chances of its attainment. Such defamiliarization and distanciation combine with a general shift of focus from the epistemological and ethical concerns of modernism to the ontological puzzlings of post-modernism (what is art? life? fiction? fact?) to allow for (potentially) a greater ideological self-awareness in literature. (Hutcheon, 1983, 36)

Such self-awareness does not make texts ideologically innocent. Rather, by refusing the reader the illusion of a past or a history as

the past or *the* history, historiographic metafiction insists on its capriciousness, as it overtly manipulates 'fact' and 'fiction'. Historiographic metafiction is thus a potentially powerful mode of fiction,
for as Hutcheon (1983, 36) points out: "to change the way one reads
or perceives may be the first step to changing the way one thinks
and acts." Historiographic metafiction does not tell us how to think
about a certain event; rather, it says: "that's one way of looking at
things, now here's another, and another, and another." It suggests to
the reader that since she is complicit in her readings, it is crucial to
recognize her own position of participation in discourse. The contribution of historiographic metafiction is not to denounce ideological
perspectives, but to increase our awareness of the necessary manipulation behind each perspective. Historiographic metafiction comes
with a warning and a challenge: the reader is warned that this story,
like all others, will be skewed, and is then challenged to remain aware
of the skewing, using the skewed tale toward an acknowledged end.
Famous Last Words urges us to question histories that come with
the tag of truth, with a sense of completion, and simultaneously
warns that we must move beyond theory, toward practice, at some
point, cognizant of the limitations of our knowledge.

This insistence of postmodernism that the text—be it literature
or history—be 'situated', first, within the enunciative act itself (as
described above), and second, within historical, social, and cultural
moments of production and reception, is precisely the work of the
Foucauldian historicist as genealogist. Critics of the early Foucault
were quick to point out that his concept of the 'episteme' (Foucault,
1970) as the invisible yet controlling ideology of a period (that which
acts as both cause and proof), itself formed a sort of totalizing co-
herence, which was unable to account for change, outside of some
"cataclysmic discontinuity . . . that can be accomplished only by a
radically originating act of imagination" (Lentricchia, 1980, 200–
01). Foucault's concern in looking at history successively in terms of
'epistemes', 'historical a prioris', 'discursive formations', or 'archives'
has been to uncover the unformalized systems of thought of a past
period's *own* time, instead of trying to make sense of the past in
terms of the present. The attempt is still to 'make sense', but the

sense made is not necessarily our own. Discursive formations do not partake of universality or transcendentality, although within a particular frame of time, they are completely powerful and guiding. They do not partake of universality because they themselves have a historical being: "as a historical a priori it partakes simultaneously of the synchronic and diachronic: it rules time, but only in time and for a time" (Lentricchia, 1980, 195). In "Nietzsche, Genealogy, History" Foucault resists making sense of history by means of forces of continuity (tradition, influence, development, evolution, or origin), while reinvestigating the process of historical change in terms of the temporality and spatiality of the systems of rules that make up a particular discursive formation. 'Temporality and spatiality' may be read as 'the historical, social, and cultural contexts', which is what Foucault (1977, 139) refers to in saying that genealogy "must record the singularity of events outside of any monotonous finality." Genealogy does not exclude an awareness of recurrence and similarity, but it does refuse the practice of reading history linearly in the name of evolution. Thus, while isolating different historical moments where they engage in different roles, the genealogist places as much emphasis on what *didn't* happen as well as what did. Genealogy "rejects the metahistorical deployment of ideal significations and indefinite teleologies. It opposes itself to the search for 'origins' " (Foucault, 1977, 141). In refusing to read history as teleological, Foucault resists the traditional perception of history as linear, which privileges both the 'origin' and the subject of consciousness who interprets, and thus controls, the past from the perspective of the present.

Foucault's essay refers to (and continues) Nietzsche's challenge of the pursuit of the origin, seeing this pursuit as an attempt to capture the exact essence of things (an image of primordial truth). The genealogist, says Foucault, finds that there is no timeless and essential secret, but rather, that the 'essence' of things has been a piecemeal fabrication: "What is found at the historical beginning of things is not the inviolable identity of their origin; it is the dissension of other things. It is disparity" (1977, 142). Thus, whereas traditional metaphysics teaches us that "things are most precious and essential

at the moment of birth," the genealogist finds that "historical be-
ginnings are lowly" (1977, 143).

Traditionally, the 'origin' was supposed to be the site of the truth
since it lies at a place of inevitable loss. Genealogy turns this assumption on its head, positing that "behind the always recent, av-
aricious, and measured truths . . . [lies] the ancient proliferation of
errors" (Foucault, 1977, 143). In other words, our very concept of
a truth, which we validate by connecting it to an origin, itself has a
history. For the genealogist, "Truth is undoubtedly the sort of error
that cannot be refuted because it was hardened into an unalterable
form in the long baking process of history" (1977, 144). In short,
there is a history of 'truth' as well as of everything else. This is not
to say that there can be no such thing as a study of values, morality,
or knowledge, but rather, that this study must never confuse itself
with a quest for their 'origins'.

Because our history of Western metaphysics takes place within
a tradition of the subject as male, an attempted return to the origin
in history often reproduces or substantiates a patriarchal system.
Christa Wolf's historiographic metafiction *Cassandra* enacts a "critical revisiting" (Hutcheon, 1988, 195) of the past in an attempt to
reread the events around the fall of Troy outside of a patriarchal
paradigm. As Hutcheon (1988) explains, in Homer's presentation of
this particular history, only the patriarchal experience of war got
narrated, "whereas [in Wolf's *Cassandra*] there is an entire parallel
world of women living in caves outside Troy and it is Cassandra—
the ex-centric woman artist figure—who tells its history" (195). Wolf,
in her essay "Conditions of a Narrative" which accompanies the
English translation of *Cassandra*, explains:

> As for the *Iliad*, it was the first known attempt to impose
> a standard of human emotion on a bare chronology ruled
> by the law of battle and carnage. That standard: the
> wrath of Achilles. But the line the narrator pursues is
> that of male action. Everyday life, the world of women,
> shines through only in the gaps between the descriptions
> of battle. (233)

A different history is told, however, when the narrator is Trojan and a woman. Achilles the hero becomes "Achilles the brute" and Agamemnon an "empty-headed ninny" (Wolf, 41). And Cassandra's gift of prophesy becomes the ability to see the future by having "the courage to see things as they really are in the present" (Wolf, "Conditions of a Narrative," 238). However, because the dangers she sees and the caution she exhorts run contrary to what the men in power must believe in order to continue to war, she is not, of course, believed.

In Wolf's "critical revisiting" of Troy, Cassandra is the only one who speaks of the upcoming "woe," precisely because as the King's daughter and priestess she has a voice in the power structure. But, because what she says makes no sense within the patriarchal paradigm of war and victory, she is thought to be mad. Yet we are told that she is not the only one who 'sees' the future. Here, Cassandra is speaking to another of the Trojan women after the fall of Troy:

> Who would believe us, Marpessa, if we told them that in the middle of the war we used to meet regularly outside the fortress on paths known to no one but us initiates? That we, far better informed than any other group in Troy, used to discuss the situation, confer about measures (and carry them out, too); but also to cook, eat, drink, laugh together, sing, play games, learn? (Wolf, 52)

They are a community of women (and some men) who know that they cannot live as if the war did not exist, yet refuse to live as if war were a normal state of affairs.

Cassandra's introduction to, and association with, a life outside the walls of the beseiged palace are gradual. The story of Wolf's Cassandra is the story of her liberation, of her struggle for autonomy, from "her service to her own family, from the social machinery she is built into," to the choosing to live her own life, even in war (Wolf, "Conditions of a Narrative," 264). When Cassandra is first introduced to the community of women outside the walls of the citadel she asks a postmodern question: "How many realities were there in

Troy besides mine, which I had thought the only one? Who fixed the boundary between visible and invisible?" (Wolf, 20). It is a question she must answer throughout the novel. She is amazed by this female "counterworld in the environs of the city which . . . lived with its back turned to the palace, and to me, too" (Wolf, 48). In order to enter this counterworld, she must first acknowledge her complicity in the world of the palace. As she lies, semi-comatose following her prophesy of "Woe" for Troy, she is consumed with the pain of self-pity and hatred. Unheard, she feels deceived, neglected, unappreciated:

> How I hated them. How I wanted to show them I hated them.
>   "Fine," said Arisbe [one of the women from the caves], who was sitting there again. "And what about your part in it?"
>   "What do you mean, what about my part in it? Whom have I hurt? I, the weak one? What harm have I done all these people who are stronger than I am?"
>   "Why did you make them strong?" (Wolf, 62)

Which is to say, "Why have you participated in the logic which ascribes to them, strength, and to you, weakness or madness?" Cassandra's is not the story of bad men and good women, of irresponsible men and blameless women. It is the story of the danger of not being able to think outside of an 'us/them', 'either/or' logic. Cassandra first learns the structuralist lesson that meaning is shaped by the system or paradigm within which we look. Her next lesson is post-structuralist in nature, about the hierarchizing dangers of binary logic. She moves toward the recognition of the possibility of a third term, thinking beyond 'either/or' to 'but also'. Cassandra explains how binary logic closes down understanding in terms of her prophesying:

> We have no name for what spoke out of me. . . . It was the enemy who spread the tale that I spoke "the truth"

and that you all would not listen to me. They did not
spread it out of malice, that was just how they understood it. For the Greeks there is no alternative but either
truth or lies, right or wrong, victory or defeat, friend or
enemy, life or death. They think differently than we do.
What cannot be seen, smelled, heard, touched, does not
exist. It is the other alternative that they crush between
their clear-cut distinctions, the third alternative, which
in their view does not exist, the smiling vital force that
is able to generate itself from itself over and over: the
undivided spirit in life, life in spirit. . . .

Their singers will pass on none of all this. (Wolf,
106–07)

If, as Cassandra indicates, the Trojan people were once able to think
outside this 'either/or' logic, why could they no longer, as evidenced
by their inability to listen to their priestess Cassandra when she
prophesied that to go on with the war was to lose all? Aeneas's father,
Anchises, who is part of the community of women, explains why
the secret-police-type Eumelos has been able to gain enough power
to determine Troy's actions:

[Eumelos] is presupposing what he had still to create:
war. Once he has gotten that far, he can take this war
as the normal state and presuppose that there is only one
way out: victory. In this case, of course, the enemy dictates the courses open to you. (Wolf, 105)

Cassandra is saying that once the paradigm of war becomes normal,
then only the binary opposites of winning and losing become possible, and that neither can be read outside the concept of fighting
and death. Hutcheon (1988) points out that Wolf, in "Conditions
of a Narrative"

links both men's writing about women (Aeschylus' about
Cassandra) and their silencing of the world of women

> (Homer's) to the patriarchal structures of both thought
> and government that have created both the oppression
> of an entire gender and the potential destruction of hu-
> manity (the arms race)—then and now. (195)

But Wolf also makes it clear that it is not gender that is the determining factor, but a gendered logic. Wolf's feminism is less separatist
than postmodernist, resisting the impulse to reverse and valorize the
'other'. *Cassandra* enacts the complexity of feminist historiography,
in that it recognizes that to work without the benefit of poststructuralist theory is to be "in danger of turning into a superficial reversal
of forces of power that would leave untouched certain general and
underlying economies of meaning and history (for example, identity,
binarity, and representation)" (Radhakrishnan, 1988, 189), while simultaneously insisting on the absolute

> socio-political urgency to the feminist cause that makes
> it unconscionable for it not to claim its own language
> and through this language make its own home, thus
> redressing centuries of silence, non-history, difference,
> forced otherness and representational violence. (Radhak-
> rishnan, 1988, 196)

Cassandra's "critical revisiting" points to the historical absence, the
lack, of the voice of women. It portrays the women as being 'other'
within the logic of the Trojan hierarchy, but not without community,
not without identity. At the same time, *Cassandra* is dedicated to
the dissection of binary logic as well as of the sort of historiography
that places the male subject in the privileged place of origin. If we
were to be able to 'go back' in history, *Cassandra* suggests, we would
find communities of women *as well as* the lives of individual men,
we would find matriarchal cultures *as well as* patriarchal societies,
and all of this would take place within particular cultural and historical contexts, so that what took place 4000 years ago is no more
the privileged site of truth than what took place four years ago. That
Cassandra's lesson is not simply a reversal, a movement of the margin

to the center, is seen in a young Greek slave woman's response to the Amazon warrior, Penthesilea, who believes that the women, as well as the men, should fight to the death because, she says, "I don't know any other way to make the men stop." The young slave woman points out that there must be a way out of the 'either/or' logic, saying: "Penthesilea. Come join us. . . . Between killing and dying there is a third alternative: living" (Wolf, 118).

This third alternative, however, is to be denied the Trojans, both in their present and, Cassandra fears, in the future. As she enters Mycenae with her captor Agamemnon she realizes

> with horror that we were going to disappear without a trace. . . . No one will ever learn these all-important things about us. The scribes' tablets, baked in the flames of Troy, transmit the palace accounts, the records of grain, urns, weapons, prisoners. There are no signs for pain, happiness, love. That seems to me an extreme misfortune. (Wolf, 78)

Cassandra asks Clytemnestra to send her a "young slave woman with a keen memory and a powerful voice" to whom she can tell these stories, but is denied. The stories of wars survive; the stories of people's lives do not. To intrude upon this pattern is one of the goals of postmodern's historiographic metafiction: to provide a memory counter to one dedicated to war. This is where postmodern fiction most clearly shows its debt to both feminist and ethnic theory and art, and to their insistence on reorienting "historical method to highlight the past of the formerly excluded ex-centric" (Hutcheon, 1988, 95).

Although it would be inaccurate to suggest a one-to-one equation between feminism and postmodernism—there are too many different strains and objectives within feminism to lump them all together, and more importantly "to co-opt the feminist project into the unresolved and contradictory postmodern one would be to simplify and undo the important political agenda of feminism" (Hutcheon, 1988, xi–xii)—feminism has, along with African-American theory and prac-

tice, had an impact on postmodernism's refocusing on historicity. Postmodernism's historiographic metafiction, as well as poststructuralist theory, owe a great deal to theory which has insisted on the relationship between gender and racial difference and questions of authority and power. More to my point is the work that feminist theory, like Wolf's *Cassandra*, has done toward developing "the postmodern valuing of the margins and the ex-centric as a way out of the power problematic of centers and of male/female oppositions" (Hutcheon 1988, 16, with reference to Kamuf, 1982). This work accompanies the poststructuralist insistence on the center as a construct on which the binary logic of 'either/or' pivots, not as the location of a truth. The result is the possibility of the third term, 'and also' which, in *Cassandra*, as well as for the contemporary world in danger of annihilation, translates into 'living'.

Foucault, too, in "Nietzsche, Genealogy, History," resists seeing the past 'origin' as the site of truth. Foucault as genealogist reflects on how Nietzsche at times replaced the term *Ursprung* (origin) with *Herkunft* (descent) or *Entstehung* (emergence). These latter terms are more exact in recording the "true objective of genealogy" (Foucault, 1977, 145). The study of descent is not to be confused with the concept of evolution. It does not attempt to identify exclusive generic characteristics of an individual, a sentiment, or an idea. Instead of a category of resemblance, descent "allows the sorting out of different traits": "The analysis of descent permits the dissociation of the self, its recognition and displacement as an empty synthesis, in liberating a profusion of lost events" (Foucault, 1977, 145–46). That is to say, we have come to see history as a means by which to trace a movement throughout time which results in ourselves. The genealogist, however, calls this meaning-coordinating self "an empty synthesis," and says that through the dissociation of this self a liberation of "lost" or unread events is possible.

The term descent may be misleading if we lose sight of the genealogist's project, which is not to "go back in time to restore an unbroken continuity" or to "demonstrate that the past actively exists in the present" (Foucault, 1977, 146). Such is the duty of the traditional mode of history which traces a line from the past to the present in the name of a particular concept or object. For example, the migrations of a particular people in the past may be interpreted in the name of the linguistic system of a particular people in the present. When events of the past are presented as a means of making sense of the present, the past, seen as continuous and consistent, appears to have existed in preparation for the culture of the current historian. Rather than erecting such foundations, however, the search for descent "fragments what was thought unified; it shows the heterogeneity of what was imagined consistent with itself" (Foucault, 1977, 147).

Far from an abstract principle, 'descent' may be read in each of our bodies: for example, in our increased height over the centuries in response to better nutrition in response to changed methods of transportation, refrigeration, and a multitude of other factors, each with its own history. Or in increased deaths to skin cancer in response to changing concepts of what qualifies as a healthy appearance, or in response to a changing environment (which is in response to . . . and . . .). In Foucault's words:

> descent attaches itself to the body. It inscribes itself in the nervous system, in temperament, in the digestive apparatus; it appears in faulty respiration, in improper diets, in the debilitated and prostrate body of those whose ancestors committed errors. . . . The body—and everything that touches it; diet, climate, and soil—is the domain of the Herkunft [descent]. . . . [The task of genealogy] is to expose a body totally imprinted by history and the process of history's destruction of the body. (1977, 147–48)

The second term that the genealogist substitutes for the origin is that of emergence, which may be defined as the moment of change, but not as the final term of an historical development. What appears as a culmination, Foucault cautions, is merely the current state of things. 'Emergence', then, continues the critique of our traditional inability to perceive of ourselves as other than the ultimate achievement of time. That is, genealogy looks to the details of the emergence, rather than at the emergence itself; and what genealogy finds is violence:

> In placing present needs at the origin, the metaphysician would convince us of an obscure purpose that seeks its realization at the moment it arises. Genealogy, however, seeks to reestablish the various systems of subjection: not the anticipatory power of meaning, but the hazardous play of dominations.
> Emergence is always produced through a particular stage of forces. The analysis of Entstehung [emergence] must delineate this interaction, the struggle these forces wage against each other or against adverse circumstances. (1977, 148–49)

Once again it may be useful to think of how Derrida presented meaning as that which takes place within the space of *différance*. Within that logic we may better understand Foucault when he says that

> emergence designates a place of confrontation but not a closed field offering the spectacle of a struggle among equals. Rather . . . it is a "non-place," a pure distance, which indicates that the adversaries do not belong to a common space. Consequently, no one is responsible for an emergence; no one can glory in it, since it always occurs in the interstice. (1977, 150)

And what takes place in this "non-place," this interstice, is "the endlessly repeated play of dominations," which we lose sight of as we assign meaning:

> The domination of certain men over others leads to the differentiation of values; class domination generates the idea of liberty; and the forceful appropriation of things necessary to survival and the imposition of a duration

not intrinsic to them account for the origin of logic. (1977, 150)

Foucault's discussion of domination refuses to credit the myth of society's evolution from barbarity to civilization:

> Humanity does not gradually progress from combat to combat until it arrives at universal reciprocity, where the rule of law finally replaces warfare; humanity installs each of its violences in a system of rules and thus proceeds from domination to domination. (1977, 151)

In Walter Benjamin's words: "There is no document of civilization which is not at the same time a document of barbarism. And just as such a document is not free of barbarism, barbarism taints also the manner in which it was transmitted from one owner to another" (1968, 256). Each conflict takes place within a moment that must see itself as some form of culmination which makes sense within a particular system of rules, which, when secure to the point of invisibility, becomes a discursive formation. There can never be some form of "universal reciprocity" because that system of rules is altered through each domination. Rules can never be stable and concretized because those rules are

> empty in themselves, violent and unfinalized; they are impersonal and can be bent to any purpose. The successes of history belong to those who are capable of seizing these rules, to replace those who had used them, to disguise themselves so as to pervert them, invert their meaning, and redirect them against those who had initially imposed them; controlling this complex mechanism, they will make it function so as to overcome the rulers through their own rules. (1977, 151)

Thus stated, this is Foucault's clearest theory of change; it is positioned under the rubric of power, interpretation, and knowledge.

Change is a play of power; and power is not based on truth, but on knowledge—the one with the power to interpret the rules holds the power of 'truth'. Although rules and 'truths' are empty in themselves, they have a history, and the shifting of the rules/truths becomes the transfer of power. As interpretation is the seizing of the right to knowledge, so the will to knowledge is a will to power:

> If interpretation were the slow exposure of the meaning hidden in an origin, then only metaphysics could interpret the development of humanity. But if interpretation is the violent or surreptitious appropriation of a system of rules, which in itself has no essential meaning, in order to impose a direction, to bend it to a new will, to force its participation in a different game, and to subject it to secondary rules, then the development of humanity is a series of interpretations. (1977, 151–52)

Thus, the role of genealogy cannot be to record History, but to record the histories called the "development of humanity."

Foucault continues Nietzsche's critique of the type of history that assumes a "suprahistorical perspective" by defining that history as that

> whose function is to compose the finally reduced diversity of time into a totality fully closed upon itself; a history that always encourages subjective recognitions and attributes a form of reconciliation to all the displacements of the past; a history whose perspective on all that precedes it implies the end of time, a completed development. (1977, 152)

 Such a history "finds its support outside of time and pretends to base its judgments on an apocalyptic objectivity. This is only possible, however, because of its belief in eternal truth" (1977, 152). The way for history to evade this concept of transcendental truth ("metaphysics") is one we have been hearing for some time now: history can refuse "the certainty of absolutes."

> Given this, it corresponds to . . . the kind of dissociating view that is capable of decomposing itself, capable of shattering the unity of man's being through which it was thought that he could extend his sovereignty to the events of his past. (1977, 152–53)

This is the postmodern lesson: there is nothing—no thought, no idea, no place, concept, matter—that does not have a history, and those histories are mutable, shifting, and most certainly not likely to come together to make sense of, or to, 'man'.

What the genealogist works on then, instead of traditional history, is 'effective' history, which acts as a deflator to our traditional sense of importance: "Nothing in man—not even his body—is sufficiently stable to serve as the basis for self-recognition or for understanding other men" (1977, 153). 'Effective' history thus "introduces discontinuity into our very being" because "knowledge is not made for understanding; it is made for cutting" (1977, 154). It is made to be used in a violence of control or of change. These are disconcerting words, for we have come to think of knowledge as a moment of finality. To come to some knowledge is to come to some end, and to have knowledge or truth, is to have power. But, says Foucault, knowledge is simply a position, a moment, a space, to be used for a particular purpose which will itself be inevitably caught up in a play of dominations. There is no ultimate truth to be associated with knowledge, and there is no particular path that, if followed, will lead to unquestionable truths. Whereas traditional history works to dissolve the singular event into a sense-making continuum, 'effective' history

> deals with events in terms of their most unique characteristics, their most acute manifestation. An event, consequently, is not a decision, a treaty, a reign, or a battle, but the reversal of a relationship or forces, the

usurpation of power, the appropriation of a vocabulary turned against those who had once used it, a feeble domination that poisons itself as it grows lax, the entry of the masked 'other'. (1977, 154)

An event, then, takes place within the 'non-moment' of difference, and becomes the place of change. An event is violence done to the status quo.

'Effective' history, the *acknowledged* and injust "affirmation of knowledge as perspective" (1977, 156), works within historiographic metafiction as historical details are skewed, rearranged, and falsified as a way to show the caprice of recorded history and, as Hutcheon (1988) points out, "the constant potential for both deliberate and inadvertant error" (114). Whereas traditional historians attempt for the greatest 'objectivity', trying to erase whatever in their work reveals themselves, 'effective' history "is explicit in its perspective and acknowledges its system of injustice. Its perception is slanted, being a deliberate appraisal, affirmation, or negation" (Foucault, 1977, 157). The traditional historian, by invoking objectivity, ascertains that he has conquered his own will or bias, and reports history as if he were

a guide to the inevitable law of a superior will. . . . The objectivity of historians inverts the relationships of will and knowledge and it is, in the same stroke, a necessary belief in Providence, in final causes and teleology. (Foucault, 1977, 158)

Traditional history proposes a larger, transcendental Truth, that must 'out', that is bigger than the individual will. 'Effective' history, history as emergence, however, does not present or represent "the unavoidable conclusion of a long preparation, but a scene where forces are risked in the chance of confrontations, where they emerge triumphant, where they can be confiscated" (1977, 159).

Thus, the focus is on an active and violent participation in history, rather than a passive review. Nothing is inevitable in history, nothing assured. It consists of confrontations prepared for by chance. The historiographical metafictionist, too, writes of chance confrontation, of the incredible, of the forgotten. And the narrator-author within these texts is rarely guilty of invoking "objectivity, the accuracy of facts, and the permanence of the past." These narrators position themselves *within* history, not above it, or beyond it. We remember the statement of *Famous Last Words* Hugh Selwyn Mauberley: "all I have written here is true; except the lies" (59). Or the confession of one of the *Midnight's Children*, Saleem Sinai, toward the end of his story:

> To tell the truth, I lied about Shiva's death. My first out-
> and-out lie—although my presentation of the Emergency
> in the guise of a six-hundred-and-thirty-five-day-long
> midnight was perhaps excessively romantic, and cer-
> tainly contradicted by the available meteorological data.
> (Rushdie, 529)

contradicts Jameson's critique of PM

Contrary to some detractors, there is no project afoot in postmodernism or historiographic metafiction to suggest that there is no past, no 'real' historical referents. There is, however, an insistence that those referents are only available in the present through textualized forms, the documents and archives of the past. This is precisely the distinction between postmodern historiographic metafiction and traditional historical fiction, which, like traditional historiography, tends to verify truths of the past; historical 'data' are combined and embellished with fictional characters, representing identifiable 'types' for the sake of solidifying notions of the past.

Historiographic metafiction's project of presenting marginalized narrator-authors to fracture received notions of the past, however, does not exactly work to efface the notion of subjectivity within the text, as much as it highlights this notion in all its capriciousness. Historiographic metafiction often shows the whimsy of our insistence on control through a central figure's insistence that absolutely *everything* makes sense only in terms of him or her. Part of the project of such fiction is to reject the separation of subject and world. Rather than speak of the relationship between the postmodern subject and her or his world, we should speak of the subject as *of* the world, that is, of the subject's position *in* the world, of the world as *in* the subject.

As a means of departure, we may look briefly at the 'subjects' of some modernist novels, in which the force of the text's world closes in on the hero as she or he is acted upon by the world around her or him, that is, by history. Consider, for example, Jake Barnes, Jay Gatsby, Leopold Bloom, Isabel Archer: their perceived heroism is that of the humanist individual who survives or lives according to a self-defined code despite, but within, a brutal world. To make sense of their experience is to follow a path from the world to the individual, who maintains her/his importance by retreating inward, out of the reach of the forces that control her/his language, labor, life. Jake Barnes is 'heroic' in his dedication to doing things 'right', despite the world doing him wrong. Jay Gatsby is great in his absolute dedication to, and insistence on, a dream lost long before he believes it to be within reach. The image of the individual, alone, beating on against the current—valiant in her/his powerlessness—is one we see again and again in the modern novel. History swirls down into the individual—she/he is "borne back ceaselessly into the past." The result is a valorization of the role of the individual coincident with narrative closure.

In our traditional humanist frame of reference this design makes complete sense: the centripetal pattern closes in on an identifiable origin, a locus from which all meaning originates, and to which meaning returns. Based on a Cartesian notion of a central, self-identical, introspective subjectivity, that spiraling inwardness moves toward the exclusive privacy of the *cogito*, away from the world. Our interpretations of 'heroism' continue and reproduce this centripetal path by psychologizing the inner truth of the individual. Within a postmodern frame of reference, however, a centri*fugal* paradigm more accurately portrays the relationship of the character *capriciously and temporarily* (and usually self-mockingly) positioned at the center of the fictional text to her/his world, to history. We cannot deny that these characters are situated in the center: the postmodern condition is characterized by nothing if not self-consciousness. But this self-consciousness, often in the form of a metadiscursive pondering, suggests its own critique. We are reminded that the postmodern center is a position, a function. Set up as a speaking moment, it resists the weight of origin or telos; it is, rather, an admittedly artificial moment through which a particular story or history is read. The character of historiographical metafiction, as a subject position, is constituted by culture, by society, by history, and from this subject position insists on her/his central role in telling his/her own history, that is, insists on constituting as well. As readers, however, we are cautioned against wholehearted acceptance of their versions of history simply by their outrageousness. Such outrageousness acts as a metacritique.

For example, Saleem Sinai in Salman Rushdie's historiographic metafiction *Midnight's Children*, born at the stroke of midnight on August 15, 1947, is not just the twin of modern India, but insists that he is directly responsible for all that happens in India from that point onward. Yet his very insistence on his particular history alerts the reader and subverts the chances for our acceptance of this singular perspective. Here is Saleem telling us that as an infant at the end of 1947:

> life in Bombay was as teeming, as manifold, as multi-
> tudinously shapeless as ever . . . except that I had arrived;
> I was already beginning to take my place at the centre
> of the universe; and by the time I had finished, I would
> give meaning to it all. (Rushdie, 148)

Saleem posits himself as central to all the actions about him: as Cause Incarnate. While being acted upon by the "slings and arrows of outrageous fortune" he suggests that he is directly responsible for that fortune, or else that that fortune is specifically designed for him. But how can we take such claims of omnipotence and causality seriously? Do we believe Saleem Sinai when he tells us: "I became directly responsible for triggering off the violence which ended with the partition of the state of Bombay" (Rushdie, 229), or when he says: "it is my firm conviction that the hidden purpose of the Indo-Pakistani war of 1965 was nothing more nor less than the elimination of my benighted family from the face of the earth" (403)? We do not, and that denial of authority on the part of the reader is part of historiographical metafiction's project. These central characters with their magnified sense of importance suggest just how whimsical is our devotion to the concept of an ultimate truth, a meaningful center.

We know from Derrida that we may never escape entirely from the concept of center. What is possible, however, is to maintain an awareness of the capriciousness of that center—of its transience, its precariousness. The self-consciousness evidenced within historiographic metafiction results in a certain amount of 'play' between capricious center and multivalent meaning. Historiographic metafiction recognizes the impossibility of imposing a single determinate meaning on history, on texts, on history-as-text. Historiography is a poetic construct, as Saleem Sinai recognizes:

> Reality is a question of perspective; . . . Rereading my work, I have discovered an error in chronology. The assassination of Mahatma Gandhi occurs, in these pages, on the wrong date. But I cannot say, now, what the actual sequence of events might have been; in my India, Gandhi will continue to die at the wrong time.
>
> Does one error invalidate the entire fabric? Am I so far gone, in my desperate need for meaning, that I'm prepared to distort everything—to rewrite the whole history of my times purely in order to place myself in a central role? (Rushdie, 197–98)

The reader becomes the actualizing link between history and fiction, as Saleem Sinai answers himself with: "I can't judge. I'll have to leave it to others" (Rushdie, 198). Words are rearranged and history is changed.

Saleem Sinai rejects a given, solidified history and pursues a program that parallels Derrida's notion of the 'supplement', which also may be termed a

> centrifugalist way of looking at the world. Against the orthodox logic of origins he pits an unorthodox logic of

supplements, where what's added on later is always liable to predominate over what was there in the first place. (Harland, 1987, 130)

Thus, the supplement is not simply extra, but rather, supplies a necessary surplus to the necessarily incomplete, false 'totality'. The history told by the narrator in historiographic metafiction is a supplement, added on because of a lack in the original; it is neither superfluous nor unnecessary. Saleem Sinai's history is just such a 'supplement' to the history of modern India:

> Who what am I? My answer: I am the sum total of everything that went before me, of all I have been seen done, of everything done-to-me. I am everyone everything whose being-in-the-world affected was affected by mine. I am anything that happens after I've gone which would not have happened if I had not come. Nor am I particularly exceptional in this matter; each "I," every one of the now-six-hundred-million-plus of us, contains a similar multitude. I repeat for the last time: to understand me, you'll have to swallow a world. (Rushdie, 457–58)

To "swallow a world" is the impossible challenge offered by historiographic metafiction. Such a challenge not only insists on the retrieval of 'insignificant' stories, but also concerns itself with, as Jean-François Lyotard would say, "the undecidables, the limits of precise control, conflicts characterized by incomplete information, 'fracta,' catastrophes, and pragmatic paradoxes" (1984, 60). Lyotard's comments are directed toward postmodern science, but we may extend his insights to literature: historiographic metafiction produces the unknown. Is this not another definition of counter-memory?

In one sense, historiographic metafiction is exemplary of how Lyotard defines postmodernism, that is, as "an incredulity toward metanarratives." He is speaking of grand narratives such as religions, capitalism, Marxism, for example, any narrative that attempts to totalize human experience and history. Lyotard says that because we no longer have recourse to the grand narratives, the little narrative becomes a necessary form of imaginative invention. Such little narratives may be the texts of historiographic metafiction which show an incredulity to the metanarratives of particular histories. Christa Wolf's project in *Cassandra* is similar, as she imagines a 'word' that

> would no longer produce stories of heroes, or of anti-heroes, either. Instead, it would be inconspicuous and would seek to name the inconspicuous, the precious everyday, the concrete. Perhaps it would greet with a smile the wrath of Achilles, the conflict of Hamlet, the false alternatives of Faust. It would have to work its way up to its material, in every sense, "from below," and if that material were viewed through a different lens than in the past, it might reveal hitherto unrecognized possibilities. ("Conditions of a Narrative," 270–71)

So if we cannot—as Saleem suggests we do—swallow a world, neither need we swallow whole someone else's world. In response to the question of how, then, do we deal with history at all, how do we make sense of the "everyone everything whose being-in-the-world affected was affected by mine," historiographic metafiction raises another question: whose sense are we talking about? Within whose paradigm do we operate? To the charge that historiographic metafiction doesn't even attempt to represent history correctly, postmodern readers are led to ask the Foucauldian questions: first, whose history, and second, how do we come to ascribe such power to the telling of history at all? By no means are these postmodern texts innocent; they each have their own political agenda. Their agendas are counter-mnemonic; they read history against the grain for strategic purposes. Each text, each little narrative, is a local, subversive struggle.

In summary, the genealogical historical project, says Foucault, gives rise to three counter-mnemonic uses: 1) the parodic, which is opposed to traditional history as reminiscence or recognition; 2) the dissociative (against identity), which is opposed to traditional history as continuity or representative of a tradition; and 3) sacrificial (against truth), which is opposed to traditional history as knowledge. The parodic, the dissociative, and the sacrificial "employ a use of history that severs its connection to memory, its metaphysical and anthropological model" (Foucault, 1977, 160).

The genealogist's parodic history is the parodic double of a "history given to reestablishing the high points of historical development and their maintenance in a perpetual presence" (Foucault, 1977, 161). Historiographic metafiction is parodic in its insistence on presenting history as we never knew it. For example, *Famous Last Words* gives us a history of World War II with the "high points of historical development" as those that we in the present may be completely unaware of—a cabal of Nazis, financiers, statesmen, and royalty working behind the scenes.

The genealogist's history as a dissociation of identity suggests that there is not within us one immortal soul or one identity, but rather several mortal souls, and

> in each of these souls, history will not discover a forgotten identity, eager to be reborn, but a complex system of distinct and multiple elements, unable to be mastered by the powers of synthesis. (Foucault, 1977, 161)

Genealogical history is not committed to discovering the roots of our identity, but rather, to the dissipation of the pretense toward identity. Its intent is "to reveal the heterogenous systems which, masked by the self, inhibit the formation of any form of identity" (Foucault, 1977, 162). In this respect, we remember Saleem Sinai's memorable insistence that "to understand me, you'll have to swallow a world."

Finally, genealogy institutes a sacrifice of the subject of knowledge. The traditional "critique of the injustices of the past by a truth held by men in the present" becomes, in the genealogist's history, "the destruction of the man who maintains knowledge by the injustice proper to the will to knowledge" (1977, 164). The genealogist's sacrificial history deposes the subject as the holder of the truth, looking instead at the history of the will to knowledge, of 'truth', and finds this history to be complicit with a will to power. Those questions of 'whose knowledge' and 'in whose name' come to the fore in narratives such as Wolf's *Cassandra* in which Cassandra cannot be believed because she does not speak in the language of war and victory.

Historiographic metafiction suggests that to enter into history is to enter, if not into fictionality, then into unknowability. But none of the novels I have discussed allows irresponsibility. Historiographic metafiction specifically reminds us, with Foucault, that every act of interpretation is an act of domination, that a will to control the knowledge of history through the transmission of language is also a will to power. Within its own will to knowledge, historiographic metafiction 'cuts' this logic: it openly fictionalizes its own given history, and in the process subverts the concept of innocent historiography. It discloses its culturally constituted position to activate an awareness of occasionality. As Hutcheon states: "The best way to demystify power, metafiction shows, is, first of all, to reveal it in all its arbitrariness" (1983, 36). Again, we have Saleem Sinai at hand, who says of his version of history:

> I have been only the humblest of jugglers-with-facts . . . in a country where the truth is what it is instructed to be, reality quite literally ceases to exist, so that everything becomes possible except what we are told is the case. (Rushdie, 389)

If the incredibility of this fiction makes the stories dismissable, by the same token we may dismiss the traditional history these texts alter. Postmodern fictions suggest that every position should remind us of its own critique, and that we must "read and write with a sense of the greater stake in historical and political effectiveness that literary as well as other texts have had" (Said, 1983, 225). The counter-memories of historiographic metafiction problematize history and subvert meaning, but they deny neither.

6

Resisting Closure:

Toni Morrison's *Beloved*

W hat is a last chapter for? Re-evaluation?
Summation? The opportunity to wrap
everything up neatly? Ah, closure. It is
so reassuring. Like checking items off
a list of projects to be completed. And
when that last item is crossed off, doesn't it feel good to sit back and
see what you've done? That's it. A checklist. We are familiar now
with some of the concerns shared by fiction and theory in the postmodern moment: a critique of representation, a critique of subjectivity, an awareness of intertextuality, an interrogation of received
histories through counter-memory. So let's take a contemporary text,
Toni Morrison's *Beloved*, for example, and see how it shares these
postmodern concerns.

A checklist. What could be easier?

A critique of representation? Of course. Rather than based on
the epistemology of mimesis, *Beloved*'s narrative structure falls more
easily into what has become known as 'magic realism'.[1] A text that
is called magic realism is one which disregards the 'natural' or physical laws which we have come to see as normal. Often, it highlights
the simultaneous complexity and paucity of language, which, with
all its potential for infinite arrangements, is yet incapable of repro-

ducing lived experience. Thus, magic realism is often a commentary on the inexplicability of the world—physical, political, cultural, interpersonal—in which we live. The logic of the narrative is the logic of the fantastic, of the signifier that maps on to no known signified. In Gabriel García Márquez's *One Hundred Years of Solitude*, for example, a text which is routinely associated with magic realism, flying carpets, ascensions into heaven, rainfalls of flowers that fall so thickly they smother animals, plagues of insomnia, and plagues of amnesia are the norm. As a result, the reliance on a mimetic language to contain 'reality' is undermined: "Thus they went on living in a reality that was slipping away, momentarily captured by words, but which would escape irremediably when they forgot the values of the written letters" (53).

Magic realism is a critique of the possibility of representation in that it blurs the boundaries between what is 'magic' and what is 'real' and thus calls into question accepted definitions of either. In *Beloved* this blurring takes the form of a lack of distinction between the spirit world and the material world, between the living and the dead, between pastpresentfuture. This is a novel in which a family accepts the daily presence of a poltergeist who later takes human form as the grown-up version of the child, Beloved, slain by the mother, Sethe, 18 years earlier. The physical presence of the once-dead daughter causes a certain commotion in the lives of the women of 124 Bluestone Road, but no surprise. For Sethe and her daughter, Denver, the *addition* to their lives of a poltergeist is just one more thing to accept as 'natural'. Listen to Baby Suggs's response to Sethe's suggestion that they could move to another house to get relief from a dead "baby's fury at having its throat cut": "What'd be the point? . . . Not a house in the country ain't packed to its rafters with some dead Negro's grief" (5). Similarly, the *substitution* of the woman Beloved for the ghost-child is part of their 'reality'.

Magic realism may thus be spoken of in terms of "supplementarity" (Simpkins, 1988), which we know refers not only to an "adding to" but also a "substitution." The magic of magic realism may appear to add to, to be superfluous to, an accepted reality, but it also works to replace what is missing: the assumption is that it is the realism of magic realism that is lacking, and thus needs supplementing. Within the context of *Beloved* we could refer to the material world of a people so devastated by the institutionalized brutality of slavery that the supplement of magic to the realism of slavery and its effects was a strategy for survival. As author Morrison stated in an interview: "One of the things that's important to me is the powerful imaginative way in which we deconstructed and reconstructed reality in order to get through" (Morrison, 1988, 6).

Let's continue the checklist. How about *Beloved* as a critique of subjectivity? If we remember that one impetus behind this critique is the contested notion of the traditional humanist concept of the subject as white, male, and propertied, the tautological subject whose existence is verified by his innate power to think himself (*cogito ergo sum*), then *Beloved* is easily read as a critique of this concept. But that's too easy. There are thousands of texts written by and about persons other than the white male which do not interrogate the construction of and the identification of the subject. Remember Foucault's insistence that the subject is both constituted and constituting. That is, the subject is determined by, or is constituted by those effects which are exterior and anterior to her, but which cannot be thought of as separate from her being: for example, the workings of biology, economy, language. But at the same time, the subject is itself constituting in that none of these effects have existence without her. Think of the blurring of distinction between self and others, which in *Beloved* takes the form of Sethe's inability to see herself as separate from her children, a blurring which reinforces the concept of the subject as both constituted and constituting. Thus, when Paul D. says that "This here new Sethe didn't know where the world stopped and she began" (164), he is pointing to a radical example of the world as it is known/seen in the postmodern framework. The world does not stop where the subject begins. The world is in the subject and the subject is in the world.

Look also at the words of Baby Suggs as she questions her own status as subject quite specifically because some of the intertextual threads that historically and socially join within the weave of the subject have been shorn:

for the sadness was at her center, the desolated center
where the self that was no self made its home. Sad as it
was that she did not know where her children were buried
or what they looked like if alive, fact was she knew more
about them than she knew about herself, having never
had the map to discover what she was like.

Could she sing? (Was it nice to hear when she did?)
Was she pretty? Was she a good friend? Could she have
been a loving mother? A faithful wife? Have I got a sister
and does she favor me? If my mother knew me would
she like me? (140)

Baby Suggs's questions serve to situate her notion of subjectivity
within a narrative restatement of intertextuality. Each individual, as
text, "is woven entirely with citations, references, echoes, cultural
languages" (Barthes, 1971, 160). For Baby Suggs the citations, references, echoes, and cultural languages that she misses—could she
sing? could she have been a faithful wife?—make up a missing map
which would allow her "to discover what she was like." Baby Suggs
defines her own subjectivity as "the self that was no self."

Despite the sadness at the center of Baby Suggs, despite the shorn
intertextual threads which unshorn would have run through children,
through ancestors, through countless cultural codes, Baby Suggs is
not that impossible thing, the entity which exists outside of intertextuality. She is given meaning by, among an infinite number of
things, a son, a daughter-in-law, a community—within which she is
"Baby Suggs (holy)"—and a history not of her own choosing, but
formative nonetheless. In fact, this is much of *Beloved*'s insistence:
that many of the cultural intertextual threads assumed to have been
shorn by slavers and slavery run through each African-American. The
concept of intertextuality may not contain the notion that we can
sort out and trace each citation, reference, echo, or cultural language
that, when woven together, constitute a particular subject at a particular moment; nonetheless, each echo may play a meaningful role.

Discussed in terms of Baby Suggs, the notion of intertextuality
is imbued with the notion of received, as well as unknown, histories.

Thus, the checklist continues. May we read *Beloved* as counter-memory? Although one critic has suggested that *Beloved* "is so grounded in historical reality that it could be used to teach American history classes" (Horvitz, 1989, 157), the question is quickly raised: "Whose historical reality?" But it's a rhetorical question only—this is a chapter in the mostly untold history text of slavery and its immediate effects upon African-Americans, and of the "sixty million and more" Africans who could not tell their history because they died in captivity in Africa or on slave ships. Obviously, this is reading history against the grain of the histories of slavery and reconstruction in the South as presented by the texts of the dominant white culture.

Perhaps the most obvious critique here of traditional history in the form of counter-memory is the blurring of pastpresentfuture. There is nothing in *Beloved* that denies the past, nor negates a future, although for Sethe the future had been "a matter of keeping the past at bay" (42). Rather, *Beloved* is a resistance to the strict linearity of history. Think of how Sethe explains "rememory" to Denver and in the process warns her of a past that waits dangerously for her:

> Where I was before I came here, that place is real. It's never going away. Even if the whole farm—every tree and grass blade of it dies. The picture is still there and what's more, if you go there—you who never was there—if you go there and stand in the place where it was, it will happen again; it will be there for you, waiting for you. So, Denver, you can't never go there. Never. Because even though it's all over—over and done with—it's going to always be there waiting for you. (36)

Nothing dies because the rememory is like intertextuality—threads that reach back and across and through lives, weaving a tissue of pastpresentfuture and providing the network through which we construct meaning. Rememory is thus the intertextual nexus through which this particular counter-memory is made possible.

Wait.

What's that? No, don't stop now. This checklist thing is going so smoothly.

But listen.

Every act of interpretation is a domination. A will to control the knowledge of history through the transmission of language is also a will to power.

That's right. Chapter 5 on counter-memory. So perhaps I should mention that the history told by Morrison in *Beloved* is also a will to power: a strategy to allow a people to be the subject of its own history, not as marginalized 'others', not as addenda. And although we know by now the attendant problems and obstacles to this type of history-telling, we also know that it is politically imperative that those who have historically been seen by a dominant culture as 'other' claim their subjectivity and their history.

But somehow that doesn't stop the echo: *Every act of interpretation is an act of domination.* No, we need to bring this one closer to home.

We need to look at the interpretations I've been offering thus far in this chapter and to deconstruct what has been said, for example, about *Beloved* as a critique of representation and of subjectivity. You see, what I did was to make it all too easy. Nothing about post-modernism allows for the simple mapping on of theory onto practice for the sake of convenience and closure. Yes, we constantly think in terms of patterns and structures: we are a meaning-making people. But the tools we have learned to use in this text are just that: tools designed to be used self-critically, to allow us to ask questions, not to board up and hammer shut interpretations. What's up is a call for caution and responsibility and *self-awareness* (there it is again—but that's the postmodern) in the interpretations we put on any text, in this case, onto *Beloved*. How then is the interpretation of *Beloved* that I have been presenting a domination?

To begin with, by introducing the term magic realism in reference to *Beloved*'s blurring of boundaries between the spirit world and the material world, haven't I assumed that the spirit world is the magic part (lesser than) and the material world is the 'real' part (the center). Doesn't the term magic realism itself reassert the epistemology of representation?: There is a real world accessible to us through language after all! The 'real' becomes more notable and thus empowered by its inversion. The fantastic becomes a foil against which reality takes on unexpected intensity. Look at the solidifying role language plays in the label itself: magic realism, *not* real magic. Realism is once again asserted as the thing itself; magic is simply the modifier that butts up against, pushes, nudges, and perhaps shakes the noun.

So, is magic realism a successful postmodern strategy of questioning the concept of mimetic representation, a strategy of destabilization? Is it a crowbar prying open the structure of representation? Is that the creaking of a structure undermined we hear, or is it the sound of our own strain as we work against the immovable? Well, which is it? Or is it something else entirely? A third option? More immediately, how has this argument played itself out in my interpretations of *Beloved* thus far? Is it possible that by labeling *Beloved* a magic realist text, by positing a 'real' way of reading as opposed to the 'magic' of *Beloved*, that I have proposed a potentially ethnocentric, it not racist, reading?

What, for example, are some of the assumptions behind even thinking of this novel as fantastic? What paradigm are we working within when we say that the most outstanding feature of this book is the blurring between the boundaries of the spirit world and the material world? between pastpresentfuture? when we suggest, as did some of the book's reviewers, that Morrison's book is lessened by the imposition of the spirit world on the material world?[2] So when we ask, well, whowhat *is* Beloved, real or ghost, shouldn't we be willing to acknowledge the ideology behind the question which defines for itself and for others what is to be 'real' or 'natural'? It is a Eurocentric logic, and not the logic of *Beloved*. Listen to Toni Morrison as she discusses the book:

> [Beloved] is a spirit on one hand, literally she is what Sethe thinks she is, her child returned to her from the dead. And she must function like that in the text. She is also another kind of dead which is not spiritual but flesh, which is, a survivor from a true, factual slave ship.

She speaks the language, a traumatized language, of her
own experience, which blends beautifully in her questions and answers, her preoccupations, with the desires
of Denver and Sethe. So that when they say "What was
it like over there?" they may mean—they do mean—
"What was it like being dead?" She tells them what it
was like being where she was on that ship as a child.
Both things are possible, and there's evidence in the text
so that both things could be approached, because the
language of both experiences—death and the Middle Passage—is the same. Her yearning would be the same, the
love and yearning for that face that was going to smile
at her.

The gap between Africa and Afro-America and the
gap between the living and the dead and the gap between
the past and the present does not exist. It's bridged for
us by our assuming responsibility for people no one's
ever assumed responsibility for. They are those that died
en route. (1988, 5)

On the one hand, then, the merging of the spirit and the material
world is a rhetorical strategy, a means of presenting a story, a history,
that has not been lost, but has not been told. On the other hand, it
is quite clearly a belief in, and the attempt to *represent* a certain way
of thinking through language. The appearance of the slain child as
the woman Beloved, says Morrison: "was not at all a violation of
African religion and philosophy; it's very easy for a son or parent or
a neighbor to appear in a child or in another person" (1988, 6).
Marsha Jean Darling explains it this way:

Black people in *Beloved* constantly negotiate a physical
and spirit world. . . . In the African tradition, religion
and life were inextricably linked in practical as well as
esoteric ways. Sethe's world was deeply inscribed with a
concrete understanding of traditional African religion
and its beliefs about mother's right, communality and

the continuum that linked ancestors and unborn spirits with the incarnate; her consciousness reflects this deeply rooted cultural pattern. (1988, 5)

And again from Morrison, who here is discussing her novel, *Song of Solomon*, speaking of the

> construction of the book and the tone in which I could blend the acceptance of the supernatural and a profound rootedness in the real world at the same time with neither taking precedence over the other. It is indicative of the cosmology, the way in which Black people looked at the world. We are very practical people, very down-to-earth, even shrewd people. But within that practicality we also accepted what I suppose could be called superstition and magic, which is another way of knowing things. But to blend those two worlds together at the same time was enhancing, not limiting. And some of those things were "discredited knowledge" that Black people had; discredited only because Black people were discredited therefore what they *knew* was "discredited." (1984, 342)

Granted, we know that authorial intention does not limit interpretation, that omniscience is itself a fiction, and that each text takes on unforeseen valences. Nonetheless, what becomes increasingly clear is that we must always bear in mind that our own individual theoretical strategies, even when used to critique 'taken-for-granted' truths (about representation, language, subjectivity, for example), must themselves be located within a certain paradigm, a certain historical moment, in response to a particular "knowledge" or set of assumptions.

In other words, a way of thinking that insists on the deconstruction of unquestioned ideology, is itself an ideological stance. And despite all the deconstruction of the subject as self-determining individual, the subject of poststructuralist discourse is still most often perceived as singular. When we acknowledge that within the post-modern moment local 'truths' used for specific purposes have replaced an acceptance of Absolute Truths which struggle for dominance, we need to remember that those local truths also skirmish for dominance. None of it works if we fail to maintain *the awareness of 'being-within' a way of thinking that is crucial to postmodern thought.*

One thing that all this 'awareness' means is that as thinkers we need to hold in our minds a space for interpretations that are other than ours. Not that all interpretations are equal. The deconstruction that takes place within the postmodern moment is intensely rigorous as it searches for the blindnesses and the contradictions in our logic. This is the tension that powers postmodernism: the awareness that while each interpretation is a domination (with its accompanying drive for closure), the space allowed for varied interpretations is a movement toward openness. The space opened up when interpretations are local and provisional may become the space for dialogue. Thus, the call for caution that to interpret is to dominate is not a call for passivity or inactivity. It is not an excuse to throw up our hands and say, well then, what's the use. It is the insistence that we acknowledge our own agendas, our own histories, our own subject positions as we interpret texts, and simultaneously acknowledge the potential for the logic of other interpretations. The next move will be crucial: how do we use our interpretations in association with, in competition against, in mutual interaction with the interpretations of others?

This is all not to suggest that the interpretations I have posed thus far concerning *Beloved* (as containing a critique of subjectivity, of representation, an examination of intertextuality, or a presentation of counter-memory) are without basis. *Beloved* is, of course, an Af-*rican-American* text as well as an *African*-American text, and thus must partake of the Eurocentric (or Anglocentric) tradition. Nor is this to say that there are not African-American poststructuralists. Or that there are not African-American postmodernists. Or that *Beloved* is not replete with postmodern moments.

But what must have become clear in the preceding chapters is that the critiques and maneuvers of critical thought within the post-modern moment are in response to a very specific history of Western metaphysical logic. The contemporary critical theory that I have presented in this text is, for the most part, part of a Eurocentric tradition. Quite possibly, the intertextual threads that make up the fabric of an African text (or Chinese, or Native American texts, for example) simply run in other directions, through a history that I do not know, within a logic unfamiliar to the history of my logic.

For example, look again at what I have presented as a critique of subjectivity in *Beloved*. Remember how in the Introduction to this text I mentioned that one of the claims laid against the post-structuralist critique of the concept of pure subjectivity comes from the essentialist feminist perspective which finds it politically misguided, even disastrous, to critique that which women have historically been denied: the status of subject in her own right. How much more destructive might such a critique be for a people who have been historically objectified by a dominant culture? Look again at the earlier discussion of Baby Suggs's listing of the absences in her life and her own suggestion that these absences constituted a self that was no self. Notice now that despite the list of missing factors that should go toward constituting the self as subject, that it is impossible to read *Beloved* without recognizing Baby Suggs (holy) or Sethe or Stamp Paid or any of the characters as anything other than subjects of their own experience.

Nothing in the logic of *Beloved* suggests that its people are the 'other' to the dominant white culture's subjects. Again, listen to Morrison:

> Now that Afro-American artistic presence has been "discovered" actually to exist, now that serious scholarship has moved from silencing the witnesses and erasing their meaningful place in and contribution to American culture, it is no longer acceptable merely to imagine us and imagine for us. We have always been imagining ourselves. We are not Isak Dinesen's "aspects of nature,"

nor Conrad's unspeaking. We are the subjects of our own narrative, witnesses to and participants in our own experience, and, in no way coincidentally, in the experience of those with whom we have come in contact. We are not, in fact, "other." We are choices. And to read imaginative literature by and about us is to choose to examine centers of the self and to have the opportunity to compare these centers with the "raceless" one with which we are, all of us, most familiar. (1989, 8–9)

Granted, the text that is *Beloved* does not allow the logic of the subject as determined by skin color, or by sex, but ultimately its most resonant line, the line that closes Sethe's story, sings, shouts, insists on the primacy of, knowledge of, claiming of, the self: "You your best thing, Sethe. You are," says Paul D (273).

What we have in *Beloved* is not only a study of the constitution of subjectivity by those effects that precede and flow out of the subject, but equally, an examination of the subject as constituted by absence. Remember Baby Suggs's questions. Questions about absence. Look at Sethe, constituted at least in part by the absences in her life: lost children, lost husband, the absence of freedom, and back further still, the absence of a mother who was a cloth hat at the end of the row, a brand under a breast, who is moving away even in the recollection of, because this recollection is also of feared abandonment—a mother killed because she was trying to escape? leaving her daughter? leaving Sethe? And more, much more. The absence of a language, a culture, a world unknown until an association of words, a smell, and another memory come together, and she finds herself "remembering something she had forgotten she knew" (61): "What Nan told her she had forgotten, along with the language she told it in. The same language her ma'am spoke, and which would never come back. But the message—that was and had been there all along" (62).

The message is of a past, distilled through an African language Sethe knew, knows, cannot remember, but rememorys: that Sethe's mother "threw away" the children "[w]ithout names" that were the result of a procession of rapes by white men, but that she, Sethe, was the daughter of the black man Sethe around whom her mother had put her arms. An owning, a claiming. Again Sethe's subjectivity is reinforced by absence, by the absence of the offspring that Sethe's mother did not recognize as subjects.

And perhaps this constitution by absence is as good a definition as any of "rememory," the concept that drives the text that is *Beloved*. But it's a present absence, a remembered absence, not a void. Rememory is a combination of historical memory and the imagination, but it is more: it is access to a collective memory, another example of what Morrison might call a way of knowing.

In some ways this rememory is reminiscent of the line in Faulkner's *Light in August*: "Memory believes before knowing remembers" (111). That "memory believes" is a restatement of intertextuality, a gathering of the intertextual threads that woven together precede and constitute that unbeckoned, unthought thing called memory. The "knowing remembers" is the individual act or analysis that temporarily singles out and brings to the present that historical or collective memory. Together they make up the space known as "rememory."

Rememory not only calls upon a history, a past that is known to a particular people, it also contains an acknowledgment of its own imaginative role in re-reading, re-membering (or putting back together) the collective memory. In *Beloved* the reclaiming of the self and of history are the same. But the self is not an individual, lone, self. It is part of a community. The final assertion of the self—"You your best thing"—does not suggest that that *you* is the ideal humanist individual, the subject which gives himself meaning. In *Beloved*, and within the African philosophy it partakes of, Sethe's *you* is a reclamation of a self and an awareness that that self is part of a community, a community that exists in the pastpresent and thus the presentfuture of rememory.

So where does that leave us? *Beloved* as a critique of representation? *Beloved* as a critique of the critique of representation? *Beloved* as a critique of subjectivity? *Beloved* as a critique of the critique of subjectivity? *Beloved* as intertextuality? counter-memory?

What's it going to be?

All the above? None of the above? Some of the above? Sometimes? A better question is: What is at stake in our interpretations? What is the history or the context within which we ask our questions? What is the paradigm that governs our perceptions? Perhaps the critiques which we've discussed in this book, and which grow out of a Eurocentric philosophical tradition, as much as they are designed to question this tradition, simply provide an inappropriate interpretive approach to some African-American texts (or Native American, or Asian-American, for example). That is not to lessen the potential of the theoretical tools discussed in this text. To believe that one set of interpretive skills is applicable to all texts, however, is naive. We not only need to acknowledge which interpretive skills we are bringing to bear on a particular text, we also need to ask why. What is our agenda? What do we gain through these interpretations? And perhaps, more importantly, do we, or *why* do we want a specific text (such as *Beloved*) to be available to such analyses?

Ultimately (and ultimately refers only to the physical end of this particular book), what do all my questions in this chapter lead to?

A caution, a hesitation, a challenge, a plea to constant scrutiny of just what is at stake in our readings, our interpretations. It's not just a game. Every interpretation is a political move. Every artistic, historical, literary, daily creation, discourse, comment, is a political act. *Beloved* is a political text. So is *Gone With the Wind*. So is *Alice in Wonderland*. So is the *Bible*. Any interpretation of *Beloved*, *Gone With the Wind*, *Alice in Wonderland*, or the *Bible* must be political, because each interpretation involves choices that we make, but more importantly reflects choices that we don't know we make—those choices we would call common sense: what we've come to identify as ideology.

That's the postmodern.

It's not to say there are neither meanings nor answers. Meanings and answers are both infinite and particular. Postmodernism resists closure in that it insists that we try to constantly keep our own subject positions, history, and motives in mind as we interpret, that we recognize how each interpretation (of a book, a law, a class, a life) is also a domination, a will to power. But only one among many.

Postmodernism also recognizes, however, that we cannot live without trying to *make* sense. Neither innately positive nor negative, postmodernism is an opening, a space created for a particular awareness, interrogation.

One need not be too close a reader to have discovered, however, what my hopes and expectations are of the postmodern. I have suggested throughout that closure is death—it restricts, chokes, cuts off, and shuts down. To believe in absolute truths is to position something or someone as *permanently* 'other'. My hope for the space opened up by the postmodern is for rigorous self-awareness of our stands, positions, interpretations. To analyze why we think the way we do, and to recognize that when we make an interpretation, we hazard to discount other possibilities. These are choices we *must* constantly make and so we need to make them with an awareness of what is at stake. The potential is for diversity of thought. It is a potential which demands extraordinary responsibility. These are powerful tools.

Just one final question then.

How will we use them?

Notes

Chapter 1

1. Some poststructuralists (e.g., Derrida) and structuralists (e.g., Lévi-Strauss) suggest that proper names are really general categories of conceptual meaning—see Jacques Derrida, *Of Grammatology* (1976, 89); and Claude Lévi-Strauss, *The Savage Mind* (1966, 197f.).

2. See Jean-François Lyotard, *The Postmodern Condition: A Report on Knowledge* (1984).

Chapter 2

1. Coetzee's novel insists on a much stronger ideological critique than I am presenting in my analysis in this chapter. See Chapter 4.

2. We may remember Saussure's critique of representation through his insistence that meaning is based on difference, that meaning is arbitrary: c-a-t doesn't naturally correspond with that whiskered, four-legged animal asleep in the sun. We distinguish what is c-a-t because it is not b-a-t or c-a-p, and we speak of the same animal regardless of whether we use the words cat, chat, or gato.

3. References to Derrida's "Structure, Sign and Play in the Discourse of the Human Sciences" are from *Writing and Difference* (1978, 272–93).

Chapter 3

1. Michel Foucault in *The Order of Things* (1970) states the combination/contradiction this way:

> [A]s soon as [man] thinks, [he] merely unveils himself to his own eyes in the form of a being who is already, in a necessarily subjacent density, in an irreducible anteriority, a living being, an instrument of production, a vehicle for words which exist before him. (313)

In another sense, however, it is in man

> that things (those same things that hang over him) find their beginning: rather than a cut, made at some given moment in duration, he is the opening from which time in general can be reconstituted, duration can flow, and things, at the appropriate moment, can make their appearance. (332)

2. I owe much of this survey to Ellie Ragland-Sullivan's *Jacques Lacan and the Philosophy of Psychoanalysis* (1986); and to Julian Henriques, et al., *Changing the Subject* (1984).

3. Timothy Reiss in *The Discourse of Modernism* (1982) employs a theoretical model which has Foucauldian elements in his theorizing about change. Reiss suggests that a particular discursive model is dominant at a particular time and place and that that model

> provides the conceptual tools that make the majority of human practices meaningful: meaningful in the sense that they may be analyzed into their manner, nature, and

purpose, and may be related to one another as defining the "human." (11)

This discursive model, suggests Reiss, is accompanied by an occulted practice, which is composed of activities that can't be made sense of within the dominant discursive model, and are thus hidden. When elements from this occulted practice "start to become tools for analysis, then the previously dominant model is gradually rendered inoperative" (11).

4. My use of Ragland-Sullivan is not meant to imply that she is an 'authority' on the Romantics, or on the subject, for that matter. Rather, I use both Ragland-Sullivan and Venn as mouthpieces for some notions of the subject.

5. See, for example, Lacan's *Ecrits* (1977), Barthes's "The Death of the Author" (1968), Althusser's "Ideology and Ideological State Apparatuses" (1971), Foucault's *The Archaeology of Knowledge* (1972). See also Catherine Belsey's *Critical Practice* (1980), especially her chapter "Addressing the Subject," for further discussion of contemporary views of subjectivity.

6. See Catherine Belsey, *Critical Practice* (1980, 60–61); and Juliet Mitchell (Introduction I) and Jacqueline Rose (Introduction II) in *Feminine Sexuality: Jacques Lacan and the ecole freudienne* (1982).

7. See Susan Bordo, "The Cartesian Masculinization of Thought" (1986, 439–56).

8. See Alice Jardine, *Gynesis* (1985, 218–23); and Gilles Deleuze, *Logique du sens* (1969, 350–72).

9. References are to Foucault's "The Subject and Power" (1982, 777–95).

10. Foucault consistently refers to the subject with masculine pronouns.

11. Foucault states that when relationships of communication are added to the domains of power relations and objective capacities (domains which overlap, but shouldn't be confused) the result is a particular regulated and concerted system or 'discipline'. By analyzing disciplines as they have been historically constituted we can see

how systems of capacity-communication-power are welded together. We can also see how different models give preeminence to particular aspects of this triad by

> sometimes giving preeminence to power relations and obedience (as in those disciplines of a monastic or penitential type) . . . sometimes to relationships of communication (as in the disciplines of apprenticeship). (1982, 788)

Chapter 4

1. See Brian McHale's *Postmodernist Fiction* (1987) for an interesting discussion of "the foregrounding of ontological concerns which is common to all postmodernist writers." McHale presents as a definition of ontology: "a theoretical description of a universe," and points out that from a postmodern point of view, the operative word here is "a": "an ontology is a description of *a* universe, not of *the* universe; that is, it may describe *any* universe, potentially a *plurality* of universes" (27).

Chapter 5

1. See Linda Hutcheon's *A Poetics of Postmodernism* (1988, 87–101) for a thorough rebuttal of this charge. Hutcheon supports her argument with examples from architecture, painting, photography, fiction, and so forth.

Chapter 6

1. See Scott Simpkins, "Magical Strategies: The Supplement of Realism" (1988, 140–54) for a discussion of the "representational bind which hampers the success" of magical realism, and for a brief

bibliography of earlier important works with definitions of magical realism.

2. See Stanley Crouch, "Aunt Medea" (October 19, 1987, 38–43); and Carol Rumens, "Shades of the Prison-House" (October 16–22, 1987, 1135).

Works Cited

Alcoff, Linda. "Cultural Feminism Versus Post-Structuralism: The Identity Crisis in Feminist Theory." *Signs: Journal of Women in Culture and Society* 13.3 (1988): 405–36.

Althusser, Louis. "Ideology and Ideological State Apparatuses (Notes Toward An Investigation)." *Lenin and Philosophy and Other Essays*. Trans. Ben Brewster. New York: Monthly Review Press, 1971. 127–86.

Barthes, Roland. "The Death of the Author." (1968) *Image—Music—Text*. Trans. Stephen Heath. New York: Hill and Wang, 1977.

———. "From Work to Text." (1971) *Image—Music—Text*. Trans. Stephen Heath. New York: Hill and Wang, 1977.

———. *The Pleasure of the Text*. Trans. Richard Miller. New York: Hill and Wang, 1975.

Belsey, Catherine. *Critical Practice*. New York: Methuen, 1980.

Benjamin, Walter. "Theses on the Philosophy of History." *Illuminations*. Trans. Harry Zohn. Ed. Hannah Arendt. New York: Harcourt, Brace & World, 1968.

Bloom, Harold. *The Anxiety of Influence: A Theory of Poetry*. New York: Oxford University Press, 1973.

Bordo, Susan. "The Cartesian Masculinization of Thought." *Signs: Journal of Women in Culture and Society* 11.3 (1986): 439–56.

Calvino, Italo. "A Sign in Space." *Cosmicomics*, Trans. William Weaver. New York: Harcourt Brace Jovanovich, 1968.

Carter, Angela. *The Infernal Desire Machines of Doctor Hoffman*. 1972. New York: Viking Penguin, 1982.

Christian, Barbara. "The Race for Theory." *Feminist Studies* 14.1 (1988): 67–79.

Coetzee, J.M. *Foe*. New York: Viking Penguin, 1986.

Crouch, Stanley. "Aunt Medea." *New Republic* (October 19, 1987): 38–43.

Culler, Jonathan. *Ferdinand de Saussure*. New York: Penguin, 1977.

———. *The Pursuit of Signs*. Ithaca: Cornell University Press, 1981.

Darling, Marsha Jean. "Ties That Bind." *Women's Review of Books* (March 1988): 4–5.

Defoe, Daniel. *Robinson Crusoe*. 1719. New York: Viking Penguin, 1988.

de Lauretis, Teresa. "Feminist Studies/Critical Studies: Issues, Terms, and Contexts." *Feminist Studies/Critical Studies*. Ed. Teresa de Lauretis. Bloomington: Indiana University Press, 1986. 1–19.

Deleuze, Gilles. *Logique du sens*. Paris: Editions de Minuit, 1969.

Derrida, Jacques. *Of Grammatology*. Trans. Gayatri Chakravorty Spivak. Baltimore: The Johns Hopkins University Press, 1976.

———. "Structure, Sign and Play in the Discourse of the Human Sciences." *Writing and Difference*. Trans. Alan Bass. Chicago: University of Chicago Press, 1978. 278–293. (Also published in Macksey, Richard and Eugenio Donato, eds. *The Structuralist Controversy: The Languages of Criticism and the Sciences of Man*. Baltimore: The Johns Hopkins University Press, 1970, 247–72.)

———. *Positions*. Trans. Alan Bass. Chicago: University of Chicago Press, 1981.

———. "Différance." *Margins of Philosophy*. Trans. Alan Bass. Chicago: University of Chicago Press, 1982. 1–27.

Eco, Umberto. *The Name of the Rose*. Trans. William Weaver. New York: Harcourt Brace Jovanovich, 1976.

Faulkner, William. *Light in August*. 1932. New York: Random House, 1968.

Findley, Timothy. *Famous Last Words*. New York: Dell, 1981.

Foster, Hal. "Postmodernism: A Preface." *The Anti-Aesthetic: Essays of Postmodern Culture*. Ed. Hal Foster. Port Townsend, Washington: Bay Press, 1983. ix–xvi.

Foucault, Michel. *The Order of Things: An Archaeology of the Human Sciences*. New York: Pantheon, 1970.

———. *The Archaeology of Knowledge and the Discourse on Language*. Trans. A.M. Sheridan Smith. New York: Pantheon, 1972.

———. "Nietzsche, Genealogy, History." *Language, Counter-Memory, Practice: Selected Essays and Interviews*. Trans. Donald F. Bouchard and Sherry Simon. Ithaca: Cornell University Press, 1977.

———. "The Subject and Power." *Critical Inquiry* (1982): 777–95. Rpt. from Afterword to Hubert L. Dreyfus and Paul Rabinow, *Michel Foucault: Beyond Structuralism and Hermeneutics*, 2nd ed. Chicago: University of Chicago Press, 1983.

Fraser, Nancy, and Linda Nicholson. "Social Criticism without Philosophy: An Encounter between Feminism and Postmodernism." in Ross, 1988, 83–104.

García Márquez, Gabriel. *One Hundred Years of Solitude*. Trans. Gregory Rabassa. New York: Avon, 1980.

Gates, Henry Louis, Jr. "Criticism in the Jungle." *Black Literature & Literary Theory*. New York: Methuen, 1984.

Harland, Richard. *Superstructuralism: The Philosophy of Structuralism and Post-Structuralism*. New York: Methuen, 1987.

Henriques, Julian, et al. *Changing the Subject: Psychology, Social Regulation and Subjectivity*. New York: Methuen, 1984.

Horvitz, Deborah. "Nameless Ghosts: Possession and Dispossession in *Beloved*. *Studies in American Fiction* 17.2 (1989): 157–67.

Hutcheon, Linda. "A Poetics of Postmodernism?" *Diacritics* (Winter 1983): 33–42.

———. *A Theory of Parody*. New York: Methuen, 1985.

———. *A Poetics of Postmodernism: History, Theory, Fiction*. New York: Routledge, 1988.

Huyssen, Andreas. "Mapping the Postmodern." *New German Critique* 33 (1984): 5–52.

Jameson, Fredric. *The Prison-House of Language: A Critical Account of Structuralism and Russian Formalism*. Princeton: Princeton University Press, 1972.

———. "Postmodernism, Or The Cultural Logic of Late Capitalism." *New Left Review* 146 (1984): 53–92.

———. (1984a) Foreword to Lyotard 1984, vii–xxi.

Jardine, Alice. *Gynesis*. Ithaca: Cornell University Press, 1985.

Johnson, Barbara. Trans. Introduction. *Dissemination*. By Jacques Derrida. Chicago: University of Chicago Press, 1981.

Kamuf, Peggy. "Replacing Feminist Criticism." *Diacritics* 12.2 (1982): 42–47.

Kristeva, Julia. *Semiotiké*. Paris: Seuil, 1969. Section quoted translated in Culler, 1981, 107.

———. *Recherches pour une semanalyse*. Paris: Seuil, 1969a. Section quoted translated in Philip E. Lewis. "Revolutionary Semiotics." *Diacritics* 4 (Fall 1974): 28–32.

———. *Desire in Language: A Semiotic Approach to Literature and Art*. Trans. Thomas Gora, Alice Jardine, Leon S. Roudiez. Ed. Leon S. Roudiez. New York: Columbia University Press, 1980.

———. "Word, Dialogue and Novel." *The Kristeva Reader*. Ed. Toril Moi. New York: Columbia University Press, 1986. 34–61.

———. "Revolution in Poetic Language." (1986a) *The Kristeva Reader*. Trans. Margaret Waller. Ed. Toril Moi. New York: Columbia University Press, 1986, 90–136.

Kroker, Arthur, and David Cook. *The Postmodern Scene: Excremental Culture and Hyper-Aesthetics*. 2nd ed. New York: St. Martin's Press, 1986.

Lacan, Jacques. *Ecrits: A Selection*. Trans. Alan Sheridan. New York: W.W. Norton, 1977.

———. *The Four Fundamental Concepts of Psychoanalysis*. Trans. Alan Sheridan. Harmondsworth: Penguin, 1979.

Lemaire, Anika. *Jacques Lacan*. Trans. David Macey. Boston: Routledge & Kegan Paul, 1977.

Lentricchia, Frank. *After the New Criticism*. Chicago: University of Chicago Press, 1980.

Lévi-Strauss, Claude. *The Savage Mind*. Chicago: University of Chicago Press, 1966.

Lyotard, Jean-François. *The Postmodern Condition: A Report on Knowledge*. Trans. Geoff Bennington and Brian Massumi. Minneapolis: University of Minnesota Press, 1984.

McCaffery, Larry, ed. *Postmodern Fiction: A Bio-Bibliographical Guide*. New York: Greenwood Press, 1986.

McHale, Brian. *Postmodernist Fiction*. New York: Methuen, 1987.

Mitchell, Juliet. Introduction I. *Feminine Sexuality: Jacques Lacan and the école freudienne*. By Juliet Mitchell and Jacqueline Rose. New York: W.W. Norton, 1982. 1–26.

Morrison, Toni. *Sula*. New York: Knopf, 1974.

———. *Song of Solomon*. New York: Signet, 1977.

———. "Rootedness: The Ancestor as Foundation." *Black Women Writers 1950–1980: A Critical Evaluation*. Ed. Mari Evans. Garden City, New York: Anchor Press/Doubleday, 1984, 339–45.

———. *Beloved*. New York: Knopf, 1987.

———. "In the Realm of Responsibility." *Women's Review of Books*. (March 1988): 5–6.

———. "Unspeakable Things Unspoken: The Afro-American Presence in American Literature." *Michigan Quarterly Review* 28.1 (1989): 1–34.

Radhakrishnan, R. "The Post-Modern Event and the End of Logocentrism." *Boundary 2* (Fall 1983): 33–60.

———. "Feminist historiography and post-structuralist thought: Intersections and departures." *The Difference Within: Feminism and Critical Theory*. Eds. Elizabeth Meese and Alice Parker. Philadelphia: John Benjamins, 1988. 189–205.

———. "The Changing Subject and the Politics of Theory." *Differences: A Journal of Feminist Cultural Studies* 2.2 (1990): 126–52.

Ragland-Sullivan, Ellie. *Jacques Lacan and the Philosophy of Psychoanalysis*. Urbana: University of Illinois Press, 1986.

Reiss, Timothy J. *The Discourse of Modernism*. Ithaca: Cornell University Press, 1982.

Rose, Jacqueline. Introduction II. *Feminine Sexuality: Jacques Lacan and the école freudienne*. By Juliet Mitchell and Jacqueline Rose. New York: W.W. Norton, 1982. 27–58.

Ross, Andrew. Introduction. *Universal Abandon? The Politics of Postmodernism*. Ed. Andrew Ross. Minneapolis: University of Minnesota Press, 1988. vii–xviii.

Rumens, Carol. "Shades of the Prison-House." *Times Literary Supplement* (October 16–22, 1987): 1135.

Rushdie, Salman. *Midnight's Children*. New York: Avon, 1980.

Said, Edward. *The Work, The Text, and the Critic*. Cambridge: Harvard University Press, 1983.

(de) Saussure, Ferdinand. *Course in General Linguistics*. Trans. Wade Baskin. Ed. Charles Bally and Albert Sechehaye. New York: McGraw-Hill, 1966.

Simpkins, Scott. "Magical Strategies: The Supplement of Realism." *Twentieth Century Literature* 34.2 (1988): 140–54.

Smith, Paul. *Discerning the Subject*. Minneapolis: University of Minnesota Press, 1988.

Spanos, W.V. "Postmodern Literature and Its Occasion." *Repetitions: Essays on the Postmodern Occasion*. Baton Rouge: Louisiana State University Press, 1987.

Thiher, Alan. *Words in Reflection: Modern Language Theory and Postmodern Fiction*. Chicago: University of Chicago Press, 1984.

Tompkins, Jane. "A Short Course in Post-Structuralism." *College English* 50.7 (1988): 733–47.

Tournier, Michel. *Friday*. Trans. Norman Denny. New York: Pantheon, 1969.

Trachtenberg, Stanley, et al. *The Postmodern Moment: A Handbook of Contemporary Innovation in the Arts*. Ed. Stanley Trachtenberg. Westport, Connecticut: Greenwood Press, 1985.

Urwin, Cathy. (1984) "Power Relations and the Emergence of Language." in Henriques, et al., 1984, 264–322.

Venn, Couze. (1984) "The Subject of Psychology." in Henriques, et al., 1984, 119–52.

Watt, Ian. *The Rise of the Novel: Studies in Defoe, Richardson and Fielding.* Berkeley: University of California Press, 1957.

Waugh, Patricia. *Metafiction: The Theory and Practice of Self-Conscious Fiction.* New York: Methuen, 1984.

White, Hayden. *Metahistory: The Historical Imagination in Nineteenth-Century Europe.* Baltimore: The Johns Hopkins University Press, 1973.

Wolf, Christa. *Cassandra: A Novel and Four Essays.* Trans. Jan Van Heurck. New York: Farrar Straus Giroux, 1984.

Index

Absolute Subject: 88
act of enunciation: 149
African-American: 10–11, 13–14,
   163, 182–183, 188–92
After the New Criticism: 136
agency: 36
agent: 37, 83, 87
Alcoff, Linda: 11–12, 14
Alice in Wonderland: 192
Althusser, Louis: 1, 9, 87–88, 90,
   98, 140–46, 197
Anxiety of Influence: 132
Archaeology of Knowledge, The:
   149, 197
"Aunt Medea" 199

Barthes, Roland: 1, 15, 17, 87,
   101, 121–28, 132–37, 140,
   197
Beloved: 17, 179–193
Belsey, Catherine: 88, 90, 97, 197
Benjamin, Walter: 167
Bible, The: 192
binary; binarism: 43–44, 47, 136,
   160–62
Bloom, Harold: 132–33
Bordo, Susan: 197

Brecht: 7

Calvino, Italo: 16, 19–20, 22, (see
   "Sign in Space, A")
Carter, Angela: 1, 17
"Cartesian Masculinization of
   Thought, The": 197
Cassandra: 17, 151, 158–64, 176,
   178
Changing the Subject: 196
Christian, Barbara: 13–16
Coetzee, J. M.: 1, 16, 49, 51–64,
   76–79, 81, 123–25, 129, 133,
   195, (see *Foe*)
cogito: 84, 172
"Conditions of a Narrative": 158–
   59, 161, 176
Cook, (David): 3
Cosmicomics: 19, 20
counter-memory: 1, 16–17, 150–
   51, 175, 178–79, 183, 188
   -defined: 150
   -counter-mnemonic: 13, 176
Course in General Linguistics: 19
Critical Practice: 88, 197
critical revisiting: 1, 158–59, 162
Crouch, Stanley: 199

Culler, Jonathan: 24, 26, 30–31, 34, 43, 128–29, 132–33

Darling, Marsha Jean: 186
Darwin: 85
"Death of the Author, The": 121, 125, 197
deconstruction: 1, 23, 188
-defined: 47
Defoe, Daniel: 50, 78, 123, 139, 140
de Lauretis, Teresa: 1, 14
Deleuze, Gilles: 197
Derrida, Jacques: 1, 4–5, 16, 20–21, 47, 49, 65–75, 83, 87, 88–90, 101, 122, 148, 166, 174, 195, 196
Descartes: 84–85
descent (Herkunft): 164–65
diachronic; diachronically: 31–34, 43, 45, 157
différance: 1, 5, 16, 22, 47, 70–76, 148, 166
-defined: 65, 70, 72–73, 75
-and power: 114–15
-and subjectivity: 89–90
"Différance": 16, 50, 70–75
discourse, defined: 99
Discourse of Modernism, The: 196
discursive formation: 149–50, 156–57, 167
-defined: 149
Don Quixote: 5

Eco, Umberto: 15
Ecrits: 197
écriture: 122
'effective' history: see history
emergence (entstehung): 164–66, 170
episteme: 99, 156
event: 169–70
ex-centric: 1, 148, 163, 164

Famous Last Words: 17, 151–56, 171, 177

Faulkner, William: 191
Feminine Sexuality: 95–96, 197
feminism, feminist(s): 1, 10–14, 163
-cultural feminism: 11
-feminist historiography: 12–14, 162
-feminism and poststructuralism: 11–13, 162
-feminism and subjectivity: 85, 189
Findley, Timothy: 17, 151, 153
(see Famous Last Words)
Flaubert: 7
Foe: 16, 17, 49–64, 75–79, 81, 122–27, 129, 130, 133–34
Foster, Hal: 3
Foucault, Michel: 1, 3, 5, 12, 17, 55, 87, 97–119, 148–51, 156–58, 164–70, 176–78, 181, 196, 197
Fraser, Nancy: 14
Freud: 7, 86, 90, 94
Friday: 17, 97–119, 122–23, 127, 137–46
"From Work to Text": 17, 122–135

Galileo: 84
García Márquez, Gabriel: 180
Gates, Henry Louis, Jr.: 11
genealogy, genealogist: 1, 16, 100, 150, 156–58, 164–66, 168, 169, 176–77
Gone With the Wind: 192
Gynesis: 197

Harland, Richard: 29, 99–100, 175
Henriques, Julian, et al.: 196
historiographic metafiction: 1, 8, 16, 130, 146, 147–78 (see Chapter 5)
-defined: 150–51
-and subjectivity: 171, 173
historiography: 1, 14, 162, 174
-defined: 147